DEDICATED TO ALL UDT / SEAL WARRIORS
PAST, PRESENT AND FUTURE

◊ *Michael Jaco* ◊

The Intuitive Warrior: Lessons From a Navy SEAL on Unleashing Your Hidden Potential

SECOND EDITION
Intuitive Warrior Series :: Volume I

Copyright © 2022 by Michael Jaco
Published by the Consortium of Collective Consciousness Publishing™

As is common in a historic and reference book such as this, much of the information included on these pages has been collected from diverse sources. When possible, the information has been checked and double-checked. Almost every topic has at least three data points, that is, three different sources report the same information. Even with special effort to be accurate and thorough, the author and publisher cannot vouch for each and every reference. The author and publisher assume no responsibility or liability for any outcome, loss, arrest, or injury that occurs as a result of information or advice contained in this book. As with the purchase of goods or services, caveat emptor is the prevailing responsibility of the purchaser, and the same is true for the student of the esoteric.

Library of Congress Control Number: 2022932954

Jaco, Michael
    THE INTUITIVE WARRIOR: LESSONS FROM A NAVY SEAL ON
    UNLEASHING YOUR HIDDEN POTENTIAL / Michael Jaco
        p. cm.
    Includes Glossary
    print ISBN 13: 9781888729764 (Pbk.)

1. Personal Transformation Self-Help 2. Spirituality—Guidebooks. I. Title
    Library of Congress Catalog Card Number: TBA

Printed in the United States of America.

10 9 8 7 6 5 4 3 2 1

THE INTUITIVE

WARRIOR: LESSONS FROM A NAVY SEAL ON UNLEASHING YOUR HIDDEN POTENTIAL

MICHAEL JACO

SECOND EDITION

Consortium of Collective Consciousness Publishing
www.CCCPublishing.com • www.MichaelKJaco.com • www.UnleashingIntuition.com

THE INTUITIVE WARRIOR

CONTENTS

THE INTUITIVE WARRIOR

CONTENTS

FOREWORD TO THE INTUITIVE WARRIOR

By Brad Olsen

I've been fascinated with the idea of telepathic communications in the movies ever since the first "Star Wars" film when Obi-Wan Kenobi used the Jedi's mind trick to convince the Stormtoopers "these aren't the droids you're looking for," and they let him move along, even though those were the droids they were looking for! Maybe art does imitate life. At the beginning of the film "The Men Who Stare at Goats" there is a tantalizing proclamation that "more of this is true than you would believe." This dark comedy is based on a team of remote viewers who could travel with their minds anywhere they wanted. The opening character says bluntly, "we were psychic spies, mainly." The real life story the movie portrays was based on events that are almost too bizarre to believe. In the film, reporter Bob Wilton (Ewan McGregor) discovers an experimental top-secret wing of the U.S. military called The New Earth Army, trained to change the way wars are fought through New Age psychic power. In search of his next big story, Wilton tracks down Lyn Cassidy (George Clooney), a shadowy figure who claims to be a member of this legion of "Warrior Monks" with unparalleled psychic powers who can read the enemy's thoughts, pass through walls, and even kill a goat simply by staring at it. But is there any truth to the government's attempts to harness soldiers' paranormal abilities in order to combat its enemies? Well, actually, there is.

The quirky Hollywood production of "The Men Who Stare at Goats" is based on the true story documentary of the real-life "Third Eye Spies." Indeed, for more than 20 years the CIA studied psychic abilities for use in their top-secret spy programs. With previously classified details about Extra Sensory Perception (ESP) now finally coming to light, there can be no more secrets. The CIA and U.S. Army intelligence employed psychics to play Peeping Tom on their adversaries, because, much to their chagrin, their adversaries were doing it to us. For several decades, the Soviet Union was on the cutting edge of psychic remote viewing abilities in the task of gathering intelligence.

The quirky dark comedy "The Men Who Stare at Goats" was inspired by a real life story that most people would hardly believe is actually true, but portrays astonishing revelations about a top-secret wing of the U.S. Army intelligence. Both films bring to light the seriousness of the third eye spies watching over each other's every move during the Cold War. Following the Soviet efforts, the U.S. program was begun in 1983, on the Fort Bragg base in North Carolina. The movie then pivots to Iraq during the first Gulf War where the "Third Eye Spies" were employed in real life to gather intellegence. Sometimes the truth is stranger than fiction.

SETH SPEAKS

Telepathic abilities and seemily super human abilities are also featured in nonfiction litrature. I remember as a young adult reading several in a series of books about a disincarnate soul named Seth, who referred to himself as a "bloodless old spook," and communicated with a couple via a ouija board starting in the 1960s to eventully complete over 20 books in the following years. Seth "spoke" about several ways that future scientists would employ intuitive knowledge to advance the human race. In the 45th Session, 9:45, Seth revealed:

Hypnotism will become more and more a tool of scientific investigation. Telepathy will be proven without a doubt, and utilized, sadly enough in the beginning, for purposes of war and intrigue. Nevertheless telepathy will enable your race to make its first contact with alien intelligence. It will not at first be recognized as such.

This session was from 1964, when Michael Jaco was still a toddler! Seth didn't like to make predictions because, as he often explains in his books, there really is no future, nor past, nor present, but simultaneous time, with everything happening at once, and also, we do have free will. We create our own reality, a phrase originated with

Seth and now in common usage. By using our inner senses, such as dreams, we have the ability to make changes, and to accept or reject any given predictions. This is why many psychic readings are wrong. The individual who receives the reading, changes the predictive outcome. Reading the *Seth Speaks* series of books is fun, informative, and helps us understand the intuitive abilities we all possess. Seth continues in Session 55, also from the mid-1960s:

Space travel, when it occurs, will utilize expansion of self. Your idea of death is based on your dependence upon the outer senses. You will learn that it is possible, through no physical act, to relinquish the physical body, expand the self, using atoms and molecules as stepping stones to a given destination, and reforming the physical body at the other end.

That sounds a lot like teleportation technology as portrayed in the original *Star Trek* television series, also from the mid-1960s! Now teleportation technology is reportedly used in military exercises, along with cargo and personnel shipments in the Secret Space Program. Once again, the truth can be stranger than fiction.

DOUBLE MEANING

It can be said that nobody is born a warrior. We choose to be one only when we refuse to stay seated. We choose to be one when we recognize injustice and refuse to back down. We choose to be a warrior when we stand up after getting knocked down. We choose to be one because in a world filled with sheep, we would rather be a lion.

A warrior is also someone fighting or struggling through something on an interpersonal, or intuitive level. It can be a mental struggle. It does not always have to be a physical fight, but an emotional battle because we know in our heart what's true. The light side is coming to the foregone conclusion that what we suspected was right all along, and the dark side is the battle we all face, but in the end becoming victorious. The struggle that a warrior endures on the physical battlefield is comparable to the mental anguish and pain that someone goes through being a warrior fighting for what they know their intuition is telling them. In the end, the warrior becomes the master.

In this book, Michael Jaco recounts how his perceptive abilities were used not only to save his own life, but others on his SEAL team. Examples are how he used his intuitive instincts in avoiding roadside bombs and deadly ambushes in Iraq. Using his remote viewing abilities he helped track down fugitives like Panama's Manuel Noriega, or deposed Iraqi dictator Saddam Hussein. He describes how these are abilities we all have within us, and how we can access them if we know where to look.

As the warrior becomes awakened inside each of us, we become more intuned with ourselves and the larger world around us. The intuitive warrior becomes intensely interested in self-mastery. The life parallels of travel, physical training, and the universal mysteries take on a much greater meaning. And we've been preparing for this challenge ever since our incarnation.

Brad Olsen
CCC Publishing
Santa Cruz, CA

I took this picture the night I met with the doctor that was to reveal OBL's location.

INTRODUCTION

I wanted to keep this introduction short because I usually skim the intro myself and jump into the heart of the book. The only time I attempt to read an entire intro is if it's short or it's an obviously integral part of a book I'm really interested in. That being said, all of the information in this book is factual. I have not used "writer's privilege" to make false claims about things and events, as I sometimes see done in works that cover an author's "life events." Although I have skirted around revealing names and places at times to preserve the identity and tactics of those who are still striving to protect the lives of others, it in no way detracts from the real events of the story line.

I have used my own personal experiences to illustrate the theme of this book, which is that we all possess extraordinary abilities, one of the most profound being intuition. I believe that intuition will be widely accepted and utilized for every aspect of our lives in the near future, and I have striven to relate how intuitional abilities have saved countless lives, including my own, in combat situations. I have also related how this ability developed within me and how, once recognized, I expanded it into every aspect of my life.

Trying to relay information that is not always identifiable by current analytical processes is sometimes haphazard, but through real life stories and examples that illustrate how others can achieve the same results, I hope to have bridged this potential gap in understanding. Keep an open mind as you read this book, and you will be greeted with a knowledge and awareness that is awakening within all of us. This story is for you personally because you have been drawn to this book by circumstances which are right for you and which have led you to this point in time. I'm trying to reach you through a medium of words that sometimes fail to do true justice to real life events, but the ability of life events to mold us into who and what we are should be shared when others can possibly benefit, and that is the real reason I have written this book.

"THE WORLD IS A DANGEROUS PLACE, NOT BECAUSE OF THOSE WHO DO EVIL, BUT BECAUSE OF THOSE WHO LOOK ON AND DO NOTHING."

◊ *Albert Einstein* ◊

Chapter 1

THE IMPOSSIBLE AS POSSIBLE

The armored vehicle began to quickly accelerate as we left the last checkpoint out of the green, or safe, zone in Baghdad, Iraq.

We had just departed the presidential palace area of the former dictator Saddam Hussein after dropping off personnel that had arrived at the Baghdad airport. The road we were now on was the notorious airport highway, scene of countless improvised roadside bombs, vehicle suicide bombers, and ambushes from fast moving passenger cars that suddenly bristled with automatic weapons and raked unsuspecting vehicles with deadly armor-piercing rounds. We would see the result of these attacks almost daily as we drove by burning or burned out M1 tanks, Bradley Infantry Fighting Vehicles, armored and unarmored Hummers, cars, and SUVs of every description, some with burning or smoldering bodies still inside. Large craters and burn marks every few yards on both sides of the divided six-mile highway marked where the deadly gauntlet of the red zone, which ran from the end of the green zones of the Baghdad airport to Saddam's former presidential palace complex and surrounding area, had inflicted casualties on unsuspecting military convoys and patrols.

Governmental and nongovernmental agencies and their security details had also begun to be hit as the insurgency in the summer of 2004 began to pick up momentum and spread its destruction. The ultimate sacrifice was being forced on anyone that the insurgents deemed would further their selfish goal of complete anarchy for the fledgling Iraqi government. Even average Iraqis perceived as remotely involved in helping the new government, or just bystanders, were being ruthlessly and indiscriminately attacked and killed. Over the next several years, several former teammates and friends of mine would be wounded or killed in raging gun battles on this one road and on several others across Iraq. The best efforts of the mightiest military in the world could not control this one stretch of four lanes and six miles of highway. I was now traveling on this dangerous highway in a security detail, protecting government officials.

I had an instant of realization, as we moved over the line separating the green zone into the red zone, that I had not done a mental scan of the area we would be traveling through. Before I, or any of the teams I was working with, entered the red zone or any area of high threat, I would do a mental scan of the area to "feel" for threats. I had developed an intuitional ability over many years as a Navy SEAL, and now as a security contractor, that had helped me avoid danger and certain death, both for others and myself, on several occasions.

I now felt a strong need to do the mental scan, when an overwhelming realization hit me that we were already in an ambush kill zone and within milliseconds of being hit. I had an instantaneous and extremely powerful desire to send out the thought of love. I have learned through the study of quantum physics that everything is vibration. The actual thought of love is a powerful vibrational energy form that can impact your surroundings. I was now focused exclusively on the thought of love and imagining the vibrations of this thought form radiating out from me in all directions. It was as if an incredible urge from inside my being were pushing me to do this and do it immediately. Although I had never felt anything like this before, I had learned to trust these usually subtle nudges as they had repeatedly saved my life and the lives of others, and so because of this command from within, I sent thoughts of love out as if every fiber, every cell of my body were sending them out. For an indeterminate period of time, the feeling of the team being in a kill zone slowly started to fade and then it was gone. I quickly did a mental scan of the rest of the highway, and I knew we were safe and would make it to the next green zone at the airport without any problems.

When we finally made it back to our compound, I started to reflect on the amazing experience I had just had, wondering if the need to send out love was real or just the product of an active imagination. No sooner had we walked into our team building than we learned that an administrative group had taken an unarmored truck to the presidential palace green zone area to do some shopping at the local bazaar. As they had left the green zone to return to our location, they had been shot at by a rocket-propelled grenade, which exploded on the road close to the vehicle. The explosion destroyed the vehicle and sent glass flying into several of the passengers, injuring them, but luckily none of them severely. The attack had happened at the exact location where I'd had the incredible impulse to send out love, and within less than a minute after we had passed through the same area.

The attack on the administrative group confirmed to me that what I had felt was real. This event profoundly changed the way I viewed the world and would direct my thoughts and energy in ways I had never imagined possible. I was now on a quest to know more about how and why this event had occurred and how I could use this knowledge to help and inform others to understand it as well.

I had been employed as a security contractor in Iraq for almost nine months before this incident occurred. I had been immersed in the violence, and it had become a part of my life. This immersion had activated my intuition, which had grown within me and had now reached a new level with the newfound ability to thwart an attack through sending out the energy of love. I will explain throughout this book how I developed my intuition and how understanding and using the energy of love was an outgrowth of this ability. I will also describe how anyone can develop his or her own intuitional ability.

Before doing contract security work, I had been a Navy SEAL for twenty-four years and had been fortunate throughout my SEAL career to be among some of the most highly skilled and motivated warriors on the planet, and it had shaped me profoundly. It would come in handy over the next several years as I traveled on different security contracts to some of the most dangerous, high threat locations throughout the world. I reflected on how my training and key turning point experiences had developed my abilities over the years.

I reflected back to Basic Underwater Demolition/Sea Air and Land (BUD/S) Training in 1981, class number 116, which was when my intuitive abilities first began to unfold. From the first UDT SEAL (Underwater Demolition Team/Sea Air and Land) training class to the present, the classes are numbered in sequential order, never repeating, so that if you tell someone your class number fifty years after you graduate, it will correlate with that time frame. There is also a record kept of everyone who has ever graduated, so if someone were suspected of falsely claiming to be a SEAL, then his class number could be looked up. Class 116 had provided me with a dream that had been formed when I was five years old and saw the classic 1951 movie *The Frogmen* with Richard Widmark. I had always been like a fish in the water and was fascinated by anything and everything to do with combat and military operations even at this young age. During my SEAL career, I had worked on both coasts of the United States where the SEAL Teams are located. One such team, started by Richard "Rouge Warrior" Marcinko, SEAL Team Six, would provide me with my first combat experience during the Panama invasion called operation "Just Cause," and help me see the amazing level of teamwork that we humans are capable of even under the harshest circumstances.

On the west coast of California in 1981 when I first entered the

16

"Teams," I worked with several Vietnam veterans who were still active. I was often amazed at the intuitive and extrasensory abilities of these dedicated and highly skilled warriors. I remember one training evolution in which we were to walk from the mountains off the coast of San Diego down to the ocean after collecting a simulated shot down pilot, where we would swim out and rendezvous with a submarine.

On this training evolution, the terrain ended up being harder to navigate than we had anticipated. Things quickly started going from bad to worse as our communication gear failed and, combined with the rough terrain, caused us to miss our resupply points and times over several days. Fortunately, we had plenty of water, as we were following streams down to the ocean, but we were expending lots of energy traversing through the mountains and needed food. We had not brought much food because we thought the resupply would be a cinch, and now we were becoming exhausted from our lack of food for energy in our strenuous trek to the ocean. Late one night while waiting close to the road in hiding at one of our rendezvous points for the resupply vehicle to arrive, one of the Vietnam vets sat up suddenly and said, "I hear a vehicle coming." We all sat up quickly and strained and listened for several minutes, but heard nothing. Hearing loss was not uncommon for SEALs who had been around awhile, because of the constant heavy weapons training, demolitions, and diving that we do. This is especially true for the combat Vietnam vets, who had obviously not used hearing protection in combat battles in order to communicate with each other, and were sometimes caught in pitched gun battles just after straining to hear subtle sounds while patrolling through the jungle. So while I had been hopeful he had heard something initially, as I thought about it while listening, I figured I would likely hear something long before he would, as I was still fairly new to the teams and still had good hearing. The rest of us started lying back down after a few minutes, and I thought to myself that this guy could barely hear, as it is, and he must be imagining noises. After several more minutes, I was about to doze again when a truck came barreling around the corner just down the hill from where we were. The others and I hadn't heard it until it came around the corner, probably a full seven minutes after the vet initially had heard it. He had impossibly heard it coming from miles away in mountainous terrain while in a deep, exhausted sleep.

Many more instances I would witness over the years, such as knowing where a training ambush was set up before we got close to it when no one else could tell, would start to shape me into believing in the possibility that these seasoned warriors' capabilities were inherent traits that anyone could learn. Other occurrences over the years would also shape my awareness of how we are capable of amazing things beyond the physical. When I made it through by far the hardest week of BUD/S training, Hell Week, I thought (incorrectly as I would learn with time) that all the others and I must be superhuman for having accomplished this amazing feat. How else could someone go through ten times what the normal human could physically withstand? Hell Week was a week of back-to-back arduous physical evolutions in which you had to stay awake the entire time, except for three sessions of one to one and a half hours of sleep over the weeklong period. Imagine getting only three and a half to four hours of sleep in just one night, let alone a whole week. That experience provided me with the belief that we are capable of amazing physical feats, and I was provided with countless examples throughout my career to justify this to my reasoning mind and solidify this as tangible proof.

On one training evolution, we were to rendezvous at sea in our IBS (Inflatable Boat Small) with a partially submerged submarine that had only part of the conning tower exposed. We had locked out of the submarine earlier in the evening and had transited several miles in our boats afterward; then we donned our diving rigs and swam on the surface for almost a mile until we reached a designated point, where we went underwater and navigated about half a mile to a ship. Then we planted limpet training mines underneath the ship, navigated underwater the half mile back to the point where we submerged, and then swam on the surface the mile back to our rubber boats. After climbing back into our boats, we transited back to our rendezvous point with the submarine. The submarine had to keep a steady movement, partially submerged; otherwise, it would not be able to maintain a shallow depth. We had a point where we were to hook our boat to a buoy that was positioned on the submarine so that we could lock back into the submarine without it having to surface and expose us all. This buoy was positioned over the lock-in/lockout chamber, and we would use it to swim down a line that was right at the opening to the chamber. Unfortunately, on this dark night, with only a couple of hours until dawn, the buoy was slightly below the surface, and no matter how hard we tried, we could not get positioned to attach our bow line to it. After a full night in cold water in the middle of winter, we were all spent and at our wits' end as to what to do.

Finally, in frustration, one of our guys decided to take the line and swim to the buoy being dragged just out of reach below the surface, moving at several miles an hour. We all looked at our teammate as he jumped in, knowing that this was an impossible task that not even an Olympic swimmer of the highest caliber could accomplish, but through an amazing show of determination and belief, he did the impossible and hooked our line, and we were able to complete our training mission.

I would repeatedly see and experience many incredible feats of superhuman physical endurance and capabilities over my many years as a SEAL. One of the most amazing ones was when I returned to BUD/S as an instructor in our infamous first phase of training that contained Hell Week. Having gone through this training was an amazing experience, but coming back and witnessing this training was even more amazing.

As I've said, when I made it through Hell Week, I thought that those of us who made it must all be gifted with superhuman abilities, whereas the others quit because they either felt that it was too much for them or they were overwhelmed by the constant challenges and were therefore not superhuman. In hindsight, this was an egotistical belief, but one that many young warriors have until they are humbled and gain maturity over the years. Over the next few years, I was to learn that everyone has the inherent ability to accomplish far beyond what we collectively consider possible.

I had returned to BUD/S as an instructor after gaining combat experience and serving over half my career until that point in the SEAL Teams. I had reached what many felt was the pinnacle of being a SEAL, with a tour to SEAL Team Six (the top tier antiterrorist team), and had not taken a shore duty break in over half my career. I had loved being on the go and serving with exceptional professionals and was skeptical if I could handle the slower pace of shore duty. Over the next few years as an instructor, I would end up setting a pace that would rival my busiest years as an operator. I would take the knowledge I had culled from the Teams over more than a decade and focus it on developing future warriors. I would do it with a passion, focus, responsibility, and with the kind of high level of teamwork that had created the SEAL Teams to begin with.

My first glimpse of a Hell Week from the other side was shocking. The things we go through in this week are impossible to describe. You can see it on the Discovery Channel series *Navy Seals Buds Class 234*, watch any one of several Navy SEALS BUDS Training Hell Week videos on YouTube, or read about it in dozens of different books, but to actually experience it firsthand and then witness it is beyond logical comprehension, and words fail to do it justice.

I was even further impressed with what happens in this week to give the students a glimpse of what they are capable of physically, mentally, and psychologically, and how team effort can multiply manifold the collective individuals' abilities. I realized now why the instructors had done all the things that they had done during training, and my respect and admiration for them increased tenfold.

During my time as an instructor, I would come to understand how the first several weeks of BUD/S training shape us and lay the solid foundations of character that would carry us throughout our entire SEAL careers and into later life. Once I realized this and saw the tremendous impact that this training was having on future warriors, my resolve and determination to do the best job that I could possibly do was set. In fact, I had been taught throughout my career to leave a place better than I found it, and I was now determined to apply the utmost of my abilities to maintaining this philosophy while at BUD/S as an instructor.

As instructors, we would learn how to work as a team to safely push the trainees to the limits of human endurance and far beyond. Before a particular evolution, we would come up with an operational plan on how we wanted to stress a particular class that perhaps was weak in teamwork. We would devise a creative plan on how to work within the scheduled evolution to stress teamwork and cooperation among the entire class, to the point where they encountered difficulty, and then worked through that sticking point to form a tighter, more cooperative team. I became quite proficient in reading a class and knowing when and how far to push to gain the maximum training value. One tactic was to exhaust the students through some type of arduous physical training (PT), such as log PT. Log PT is performed with telephone poles weighing a couple hundred pounds and requires all seven men in a boat crew or team to participate to a high degree. If one person slacked off for even a moment, then the whole team suffered by having to take up that person's portion of the log's weight. For instance, while holding the log over their heads as a boat crew of seven men, every person was carrying the rough equivalent of 30 pounds. Imagine holding a thirty pound dumbbell over your head for several minutes and then having that weight increased alternately over time by two to five pounds. As instructors, we were constantly on the lookout for people who didn't pull their weight or work as a team. Sometimes if a boat crew or several boat crews were not meeting the pace set by the instructors, then the whole class would be put through even more physically demanding exercises than they were already being exposed to.

I remember one log PT evolution during a Hell Week wherein I was running the day shift, which was traditionally the easier shift for the students. Instructor teams would work one of three eight-hour shifts during a twenty-four hour period during Hell Week. During this week, we had an author, Doug Waller, who had come to observe our BUD/S Hell Week with the intention of writing about the event in a book. His book, published in 1994, was called *The Commandos: The Inside Story of America's Secret Soldiers*. An article also appeared in *Newsweek* with excerpts just before the book was released.

This was a new push by the SEAL Teams to help in recruiting new SEAL hopefuls. Up until this point in our history, we had rarely allowed anyone outside of our community a glimpse into our world and never at Hell Week. I had talked to Doug before and during Hell Week and was pleased that he was a genuine guy who really wanted to write a credible and accurate account of the week.

Doug's initial intention was to try and stay up with the class for the entire week and only sleep when they slept. He ran out of steam by the second day and had to go and get some sleep. Of course, he was just following the class around and observing, not doing the constant, arduous physical training, so this gives you an idea of how demanding this week is. When Doug left, exhausted, for several hours of sleep during the second day, thinking he wouldn't miss anything, he was sadly mistaken.

As I said earlier, I had become quite proficient in motivating the students to give them maximum training value. This expertise also included knowledge of how to put the students in situations that would provide the weak links, or people who didn't have the intense desire and fierce determination required to succeed, with the proverbial last straw and help them decide they wanted to quit. The SEAL Teams are an elite Special Forces unit and, as instructors, we knew we were the gatekeepers to the teams; our teammates relied on us to send them only exceptional individuals, so we took our job very seriously. Many think that an instructor's job is just to be sadistic and make the students' lives miserable. This could not be further from the truth. Personally, I'm one of the nicest people you could ever meet. I take no pleasure whatsoever in causing pain and suffering, but I think Hell Week is necessary. If I simply told you to stay up for the week with no sleep, do one extremely arduous physical evolution after another, and mold yourself into a team with your fiercely individualistic fellow students, and then I walked away and came back at the end of the week, do you think that you would accomplish it?

It actually takes a lot of demanding work on the part of the instructors to also work as a team, constantly scan the class for safety during dangerous evolutions, motivate students who are having a hard time digging deeper, give guidance and instruction, and have the creativity to come up with challenging and valuable evolutions that will get the most value for the allotted time. Now that Doug was gone for a little nap and not looking over our shoulders, it was time to put total focus on the task at hand and unleash our full creative potential. When we came on shift, we did the usual greeting by having the students get wet in the cold Pacific Ocean with their training uniforms on, and then get covered in sand. This was always a timed evolution with a time that was close to impossible so that few if any students would complete the task in the required time. I would send them back and forth to the surf zone to get wet and sandy for twenty to thirty minutes. Imagine plunging into water so cold it takes your breath away and causes your body to instantly start to shiver trying to warm itself. Think of the mental discipline to constantly push yourself when you think that you can go no further but know that you must to accomplish your ultimate goal. Or the determination you need to continue when you know that the evolution is a mind game designed to challenge your patience. You then sprint out of the water to the beach and, throwing yourself down, roll around so that your entire body, including your face and hands, is coated with gritty sand that clings to your every surface; then you sprint back to the position, where an instructor stands looking at a stopwatch, only to learn you were too late and must do it again. All the while, instructors with bullhorns are hovering on the periphery, shouting threats of even more challenging evolutions for those who aren't giving 110 percent. Sometimes they dart into the melee like a shark to single out a slow or relatively dry and sand-free student for special one-on-one attention. When one student fails, everyone has to complete the evolution again and again.

After about twenty minutes of this, we moved on to whistle drills, which consisted of one to three whistle blasts; one whistle would require the students to instantaneously drop to the ground, assume the prone position, cover their ears, and cross their legs to simulate protecting themselves from an explosion. This required an instant, unthinking response, no matter what location or position they were already in. The second whistle blast would prompt them to start crawling on their bellies to the sound of the whistle, which would constantly be moving back and forth over the twenty-foot sand berms along the shoreline. The third whistle blast would prompt them to jump instantly to their feet. I alternated between the three whistle blasts for the next twenty minutes while I quickly traversed the berms all the way to the location of the logs used in log PT.

I gave the final three whistle blasts and informed each boat crew they were to grab a log. They were now to start what is arguably the most arduous physical training evolution in BUD/S after being pounded for the last forty minutes with nonstop physical activity. The students had also not slept for over forty-eight hours at this point and had been doing constantly shifting and physically demanding activities ever since the start. I quickly formed the class into two rows, now with their logs, and proceeded with the hardest of all the log movements. Twelve count log PT started on count one and ended on count one. The students would start squatted down with the log on their left side, and with their right arm over the top of the log and their left underneath their logs for count one; for count two, they would stand straight up, lifting the log cradled in their arms to their left hips; at count three, they would lift the log to their left shoulders, and at count four would move the log into an overhead press that would sometimes be halted while the students squirmed and grimaced with the heavy weight extended for long periods of time. At count five, they would transfer the log to the opposite shoulder, at six they would shift it to the opposite hip, and then to the opposite side on the ground at seven. At eight, they lifted the log back to the hip just left, and at nine back to the same side shoulder. Ten would be another overhead press, eleven back to the opposite shoulder just left, twelve back to the starting hip, and at one they would return to the starting position. To keep the students thinking after they had gotten into a zombie rhythm, which often happens to people who have not slept for several days of intense physical endurance, I would switch up the count; for instance, I might call nine after the ten count, instead of eleven. This would cause a ripple in the logs throughout the group as some were paying attention to the count and tried to go back to the right shoulder and others were still in the mindless zombie mode and were still trying to go with the natural procession of numbers and muscle memory. This inattention to detail would cause the group to have to pay and go into the extended arm position for an excruciatingly long time for the muscles. We would then continue the count, and after half an hour of this one exercise alone, we moved on to other log PT exercises. After another hour of running through several different exercises, such as sit- ups with the log on their chests, we decided to mix things up and move on to log races.

The day was warming up, and the southern California sun can really warm things up, even in winter, especially if you're running around on the beach, kicking up choking dust with a two- hundred- pound log in tow. I was thinking of a way to be creative, and after another half hour of running log races, the thought struck me to take the log PT into the ocean. The hot, dry logs started soaking up the water right away, and the relief the hot, tired students felt from the initial soaking was quickly being replaced by shivering cold and an even heavier log. I had them work the logs for a while in chest-deep water as the wave swells came in and almost covered their heads. This, I could see, was starting to make some of them uncomfortable. I felt I had found what I was looking for to put the class in a position to flush out the borderline students. I would always look for opportunities within evolutions to push the students to a point where they felt uncomfortable and unsafe. We pushed the limit on our training, which is necessary for development and growth of character, but we were always safe. The perception of danger was what made many quit. Up to this point, they practically lived in the water, conducting long ocean swims, IBS surf and rock portage, drown proofing with hands and feet tied, long underwater laps in the pool without oxygen tanks, and much more, so they should have no problem at this point with anything I could throw at them dealing with the water. But there was one thing they had not experienced yet: doing sit-ups in the surf zone with the logs on their chests as the surf surged over them in the down position. They had never experienced this before, and I could see that it had caught them off guard because some guys were squirming beneath the logs in the water and getting ready to fly. They were underwater for maybe five to ten seconds at the most at any one time. But it unnerved several guys, and they jumped up from under their boat crew's logs and abandoned their teammates still struggling with the log. I remember a couple of guys who quit that day, which totally shocked me as I had initially thought they would make it through the entire training.

I learned that you could never see what kind of character a person has by looking at their outer performance. Hell Week would always identify the weak in character. This is what we looked for, and now, after pushing the class to the breaking point and holding them there for only a short time, I had found what I was looking for. This was the end of this evolution, and after nearly four hours of incredibly intense physical activity with not a second of letup, we had made the purge we were looking for. I had them put away their logs, and we moved on to the next evolution.

There's always another challenge and obstacle to overcome, but such is life, and the men who would go forward after this week would be far better for having endured this week of hell. The SEAL Teams would also benefit because these men would not look at a challenging situation and shrink from it or run away. These men had developed, knowingly or unknowingly, the ability to go beyond the physical and harness a point within themselves that allowed them to do what most would call the impossible.

In my reflections on what had awakened the intuition that was now influencing my life in a remarkably positive way, I would see this period of time both as a student and as an instructor in Hell Week as one of the main contributing factors.

"FOLLOW YOUR BLISS."

◊ *Joseph Campbell* ◊
The Power of Myth

Chapter 2

HIGHER STATES OF CONSCIOUSNESS

W e are all capable of much greater things physically, but what about mentally? What about being capable of mentally surpassing what we currently think is possible? When I started the first hand-to-hand course for the SEAL Teams, I found that we can all move into higher states of mental capability at will. Now, the word "Teams" indicates the involvement of more than one person, and that is the way it was throughout my career. I was always blessed to be around gifted and motivated people who would lead, inspire, guide, and work with me on implementing many firsts for the SEAL Teams during my career, and the hand-to-hand program was no exception.

I, like many warriors, desire to be the best that I can possibly be, and many of us gravitate toward the martial arts. When I first came into the Teams, other than a couple of hand-to-hand moves that I learned in BUD/S and some training as a kid, when I worked out with friends who knew several different styles, I knew little in the way of martial arts. I knew nothing formal from this childhood training, and unfortunately, as I would find, the teams didn't either. The only way they learned any martial arts skills was by training with different experts within the Teams that had learned on their own or by going out to local martial arts schools. While I was at SEAL Team Six, we did have a martial arts expert come in and start teaching a few of us, but just on our own time and usually after we had worked a full day.

Eventually, a few other guys and I hatched the idea to start a hand-to-hand training course designed specifically for the Special Forces warrior. I was a BUD/S instructor at the time, but I learned a system from a combat fighting instructor that the training command had hired to teach the BUD/S students. The eventual intent of the training command was to have the martial arts instructor train BUD/S instructors to be combat fighting instructors of his particular system, which was an aggressive one. They asked for volunteers, and only two of us wanted to do the training at the time. We trained for ten hours a day, for thirty days straight. The intent was to learn as much as an average student would learn in three years. This was accomplished by the intensity and immersion within the system for over a twenty-one day period, which creates habits and ingrains neuron receptors in the brain to rapidly react to conditioned stimuli. The aggressive combat fighting that we learned would change the way I viewed many different aspects of warfare and my life from that point on. I would later do another thirty-day course and learn from many top-level experts, from a wide range of disciplines, over the next few years. All of these systems had something to offer, and we rolled all the information from a wide range of subject matter experts into our own thirty-day and weeklong courses. It was during this time, while in between courses, that I was running another Hell Week shift and had another epiphany on my journey to greater awareness of our inherent capabilities for higher states of consciousness.

We were on the fourth day of Hell Week, when all the students move around like zombies. Give them a task to do and they shuffle along and perform whatever it is you tell them to do. It is really rare for anyone to quit at this point, so we usually just keep them moving and busy. All of the really hard and potentially hazardous activities were done early in the week because the students would be more prone to injury at this point. They are in a mental state wherein we could tell them to do practically anything, and they would do it. I remember a time during my own Hell Week when we had a bathroom break around this point, and my boat crew and I were shuffling along when an instructor said, "Drop and take a break." We all dropped on command in a grassy island area in a parking lot barely large enough to contain the seven of us. We had learned to instantly go into a deep sleep on these rare occasions throughout the week. We slept crumpled up, half on top of each other, half on the grassy island in the sea of asphalt surrounding us, for maybe ten to fifteen minutes. When we were awakened, I felt incredibly refreshed, much more so than when we got up to an hour or more because then everything in my body started to swell and stiffen, and it became difficult to come out of the deep sleep. The ability to go to sleep in unusual positions and times would come in handy over my career as a SEAL, because we frequently had little sleep after planning and prepping for training missions and combat operations, and we had to be able to take quick power naps at will.

We would keep the students in this zombie-like state for another full day until we completed Hell Week. It was during one of these times when I noticed this one student who looked as if he had just entered the class; it was as if he had never been in Hell Week at all. I began watching him, and, sure enough, every task that he performed with his boat crew or the class he did as if he were fresh and rested and had an abundant source of energy. I asked the other instructors if he was rolled forward in the class from the previous night from an injury. (Medical personnel evaluate the students constantly and a full screening is done every night, so there was a possibility that they had diagnosed him as unfit to continue the previous night. They had made this mistake a few times in the past; a student gets injured, and they tell him to go back to the barracks and get some sleep and come back the next morning for evaluation. They come back, and a different doctor, who is not a SEAL, finds them miraculously healed after a good night's sleep, and tells him to rejoin the class. Amazingly, when your body is highly stressed for a short, intense period of time, it can become hyper recuperative, and it is not uncommon for students to experience fast healing in what would be normally a long-term injury.) This was not the case for this student, however, and it was quite an anomaly to see someone this fresh-looking and alert on day four of Hell Week. I had never seen or heard of anything like it. I decided to investigate further and at one point actually called the student over and questioned him about how he was feeling and why he appeared so fresh. He told me he was feeling great and didn't realize he looked unfazed by the training so far. I was not satisfied and thought maybe he wasn't pulling his fair share of the burden and had craftily escaped notice thus far. I continued to watch him and was even more amazed when I saw him actually doing *more* than the other students and helping them by taking on some of their burden.

The rest of the day went on with the usual continuous evolutions until we came to late afternoon. We had an interesting drill we would run in which we would have them write a letter home to a loved one, describing their experiences so far in Hell Week. This was a way to start them on the road to learning to use their cognitive abilities with little to no sleep. We would dim the lights in a classroom, put on classical music and tell them not to fall asleep with the threat of having to run all the way to the surf zone, get wet and sandy and run back. Except for a rare few Naval Academy officers who are used to this particular kind of lifestyle, most students, myself included when I went through this training, would have micro naps while writing. Micro naps happen for a split second, but you are completely out and in a deep sleep for that instant. I remember seeing students standing with 150-pound IBS's on their heads, usually on the fourth and fifth night of Hell Week, their knees buckling and catching as they went into micro naps. Their eyes would slowly close, their knees would buckle, and then they would snap back awake as they caught themselves. I would stand in front of them and look directly into their eyes, and they wouldn't even register alarm at falling asleep in front of me. I now looked over the class and saw the heads bobbing over their desks as they entered into their micro naps and caught themselves before their heads hit the desk. All but one student, who was feverishly writing away as if he were sitting in a classroom anywhere except this one.

We usually read the students' letters afterwards to check for anything that may alert us to a mental problem, and then filed them with a log we kept for Hell Week. We had never had any problems before, mainly gibberish with pen and drool marks across the paper. The one student I had been curiously watching had written a letter to his grandfather. He was a Native American and wrote about how his grandfather had been right about what he had taught him through vision quests. He wrote that he had not believed in the old ways, but had used them during Hell Week, and they had served him well. He wrote about transcending the physical, detachment, and staying in a sort of out-of-body experience, watching and guiding himself during the tough evolutions.

This was another turning point for me as it fit perfectly with what I had also been experiencing during intense hand-to-hand training, specifically when attacked by multiple people. We had a training event called "multi-fighting" in the fighting course we were designing, in which multiple people attacked you constantly over a three-minute time period. You would normally fight the equivalent of two to three hundred people during this three-minute evolution, and I had experienced the sort of out-of-body experience that the student was talking about. Now I began to see further applications outside of fighting, that could further all aspects of a warrior's skills.

I became aware now as I was multi-fighting that I was going into these states and creating a kind of mental point within myself that I could go to at will if put into a stressful situation. This point was like a landmark, or non-physical point in consciousness, that every student was told to develop while in the multi-fight. If we saw the student struggling with the multi-fight to the point of getting overwhelmed, we would call out for them to "go into the alpha state," which was their cue to relax and go into wide-angle vision. As they repeatedly reached the point of being overwhelmed, they would learn to switch into the alpha state on their own. We would call this landmark or state of mind "the alpha state," after the brain wave pattern within the mind. We all have brain waves at any one time called alpha, beta, delta, and theta. A preponderance of one over the others will determine the state of mind you are in. Alpha states are expanded states of consciousness that are a potential state that anyone can achieve at will and at any time. Going into wide-angle vision and learning to relax can activate an alpha state. In wide-angle vision, you expand your vision so that you can see out the periphery of your eyes. Take a deep breath, exhale, and expand your vision so that you can see out of the periphery of your eyes, and you will activate the alpha state.

Not only is this essential when multiple people are attacking you, as we taught during the fighting course, but it's also like a door that opens access to higher states of awareness. This higher state of awareness allows access to information on how to deal with the overwhelming information that comes at you in a multi-fight. You would go into a relaxed sort of meditative state while you fought by going into the alpha state or your landmark. If you focused on any one thing at a time, the way you do when you are trying to analyze a problem which would pull you into a beta-dominant state, or you slipped into tunnel vision, you would stay in a beta-focused state, which is great for working at a computer or solving a complex mathematical problem; however, a beta state will get you overrun quickly in a multi-fight.

As you went into wide-angle vision, you would not only be able to see more of what's going on around you, but also be able to access the higher states of mind. These higher states of consciousness allow you to rapidly process the information coming at you. The needed solutions would flow in a way that would never happen if you were in the beta state alone. We also noticed and observed when we taught others that as they went into this state, their reaction times decreased tremendously as well.

I began to apply this information to other aspects of being a warrior, such as shooting. I had always scored expertly on shooting, but it was always in the low to middle range of the expert level. When I applied my internal landmark to shooting, my scores went consistently into the upper range of expert. I began consciously using my landmark for every aspect of my skills as a SEAL, and took everything to a higher level of achievement. When doing close quarter combat (CQC) before entering a room, I would take a breath, let it out and relax, clear my mind, go into an alpha state, and as I entered the room with my weapon to shoot bad guy targets, I would have less stress and tension and would be able to more quickly acquire targets, get my shots off faster and more accurately, and clear my area of responsibility far more rapidly than if I didn't go to my internal landmark.

The more I practiced going into this state, the faster I was able to go into it until I realized one day that it was just happening instantaneously without my having to consciously go there. I had created a habit or a neuron groove that would fire and put me instantly in my landmark state whenever I was put into a stressful situation. Before I developed this landmark within myself, I had always had a lot of self-talk that we all go through. This caused unnecessary stress and negative internal words that strangle reaction time, such as the word "fear," as in fear of failure, fear of what others might think, or fear of death or injury.

We also learned how words influence our reactions and how it is important to stay away from negative words in our thoughts and speech. We practiced Neuro Linguistic Programming (NLP): Neuro—for the neurons in the brain, which we can train through consistent practice, which creates a habit within a twenty-one-day period; Linguistic—for words and how words effect our mental states and reaction times; and Programming—for how we can use words to condition the brain's neurons to shape our reality.

We taught our hand-to-hand students the difference that words can have on their reaction time and how words could influence their overall state of mind and stress level. We taught them that the word fear was a negative and had no place in our spoken vocabulary and self-talk. The fear state itself is a negative wherein access to the higher, more creative brain wave states needed for solving the rapidly shifting realities of combat—or our everyday world for that matter—fail to present themselves to the student. If the student, through former negative self-talk or wrong physical training, should start to slip into a state of fear, which would be indicated by tension in the muscles, tunnel vision, and shallow breathing, he would invariably fail quite rapidly in the multi-fight scenario. We teach that you have to focus on going into wide-angle vision, take deep breaths, and go to your inner landmark, or that place where you have access to unlimited information. Just like you create habits by repeatedly doing a task, we taught that as you relax into an alpha brain wave state, you have access to greater non-local intelligence. By repeatedly going into this alpha state, you eventually create a landmark, or neuron groove, in your physical brain that synchronistically accesses your creative mind, which in turn accesses the soul level of consciousness, which has direct access to divine consciousness.

The words "fear" or "defense" would be replaced with positive words like "offense," which is, of course, the opposite of defense. In the dualistic world in which we live, where everything has its opposites—war and peace, dark and light, yin and yang—we need words that bring us back to the state that we are really searching for to ultimately find a balance between the two. The state of mind that we always want to be in is a positive one, and it helps to focus on a positive word; in our case, as fighters, that word was "offensive." The word "offensive" doesn't mean that we walk around with a chip on our shoulders, waiting for someone to knock it off. Ideally, we are always in a state where we are detached or balanced between the opposites, on the razor's edge as we used to say at SEAL Team Six, and if the negative feelings or words come up and cause us to move toward a negative state, then we replace them instantly with a positive. We don't give negative thoughts a moment of existence in our reality; otherwise, we would be in the state that we don't want to be in, and it can quickly cause a downward spiral, away from a positive or balanced state. This positive state is the ultimate warrior state of mind or calm mind that requires constant discipline and training to achieve and maintain.

So, as fighters, we wanted to always stay in the offensive state, and if we weren't in that state for even a fraction of time, then we were in a negative state that created all the things that would be debilitating to us as fighters and slow our reaction times. We wanted to, as rapidly as possible, move from a negative, or fear, state into a positive, or offensive, state where reaction times are increased, stress levels are reduced, and instantaneous access to creative information is allowed to come through the gateway of the alpha state, or internal landmark. Fear, or defensive words, shut this gateway, and cause us to lose our ability to respond to situations as rapidly as needed in high stress situations. Rather than activating a negative state in ourselves, we were conditioning ourselves to react instantaneously and enter into a positive state after twenty-one days or more of positive reinforcement.

We found, as we taught the courses, that most people want to fight one person at a time initially and had a hard time going into wide-angle vision so that they could see more attackers and react to multiple targets at once or multitask. Our techniques also required the fighter to constantly move or be overwhelmed, and this was also hard for most because they want to plant themselves and face one threat at a time, which is very beta state-oriented, a reflection of analytical thinking or tunnel vision. You cannot handle the amount of information—or multiple attackers throwing punches, kicking, swinging clubs, stabbing with knives, etc.—if you plant yourself in a beta mind-set and try to "defend" yourself. We were teaching them to constantly move, stay in wide-angle vision, breathe, stay offensive, and hit multiple targets on the human body as they moved, disabling attackers and making the other attackers constantly have to move to the fighter's determined movements, rather than the fighter having to adjust to the attackers' movements.

I've trained many people over the years from almost every walk of life, ranging in age, profession, fighting style, country, religion, you name it, and they have all benefited from this information in one form or another. I also find that these higher states of mind, as I call them, transfer into every aspect of my life.

The higher states of awareness that we were experiencing, as fighters and during our everyday training as warriors in the SEAL Teams, was being experienced by most, but not fully comprehended or quantified in scientific terms. I had always enjoyed the scientific process, at one time intending to become a marine biologist. I had always loved science in school and had excelled at science at different times throughout my school years. I began to apply scientific principles by quantitative analysis of behavior that I was observing, experimenting, and teaching others. I was now pushing into the outer limits of accepted and conditioned thinking with these higher states of awareness. I had learned throughout my training that the impossible means nothing if you believe in what you are doing and work consistently toward achieving your desires with a strong intention. I determined to focus on sharing this valuable information with as many people as were open to receiving it. The only unquantifiable question was how many people would accept this information.

"HUMAN HISTORY BECOMES MORE AND MORE A RACE BETWEEN
EDUCATION AND CATASTROPHE."

◊ *H.G. Wells* ◊

Chapter 3

EMOTIONS AS A
CATALYST TO GREATNESS

Little has been said and far less allowed for the emotional
state of a warrior, but it is just as important as the physical
and mental states I've already covered, and, if neglected,
can wholly affect the performance of the warrior and humanity as a
whole. Warriors/peacemakers are an integral part of our society and
are an example of the discipline and courage all of us, as a collective, embrace when overcoming great obstacles in our lives. Whether
these obstacles consist of things we are apprehensive of that must be
transcended, or challenges we need to overcome to excel in a certain
aspect of our lives, we are all warriors in one fashion or another.

Emotions, like everything in our physical universe, are an energy
vibration, and, when directed and focused properly, can be the catalyst
for achieving great feats for humanity and forming an individual's
character into one that is an example for others to aspire to. In our
dualistic world, there is always a flip side, and certain negative emotions can have devastating consequences when misdirected. Stress, when

directed in a positive way, can develop a great physique, focus your mind to great creative endeavors, or, in the case of emotions, power both physical and mental aspects of ourselves to great achievements.

During the second night of my Hell Week class, we got two guys added to our boat crew; another boat crew had had a lot of quitters and had been dissolved, and the remaining men were distributed to other boat crews that were lacking numbers. At first, I was happy to get these guys because we were shorthanded and could use the extra help, and they had excelled during the first few weeks of training, so I thought they would be a great addition. They had had a sort of cocky bravado going into Hell Week that led many of us to believe that they would have an easier time with the week than the rest of us, who always had to struggle through every evolution.

I mentioned before that you can never predict what is inside a person—what will motivate them to excel and what will cause them to pull back. Because these guys had been naturally gifted during the physical evolutions in prior weeks, they had not learned how to dig deep to survive through difficult evolutions. As an instructor, I learned that character development before the great equalizer, Hell Week, was necessary to not only teach a man to dig deeper, but also to carry on so that he helps those around him, which is an even higher aspiration. Now, Hell Week, wherein everyone must learn to dig deeper than ever before in their lives, was stressing these guys in ways they had never experienced, and they were resisting and pulling back. This emotional and mental resistance to stress was having physical manifestations, which were affecting our boat crew, as these guys were not carrying their weight effectively when we ran from evolution to evolution with our IBS's on our heads. Just moving these IBS's around was an evolution in itself that required extra effort and a need to dig deep. Our two new guys were holding us back on this one night when we were having races up the beach with the boats on our heads, running from point to point at the direction of the instructors. We were starting to fall behind, and the two guys who had joined us were trying to slow down because they were hurting. Everyone hurts during this week, and you learn to dig deeper and motivate yourself, or the instructors move in and give you their brand of motivation, which is never a fun time. The front of the boat was the toughest because of the reinforced bow that slopes upward, adding extra weight. At the point where you take the weight with the top of your head, it really pounds onto your head, neck, and spine as you run.

I switched places in the front with one of the guys who were slowing us down. If the front man slows down, it is impossible for the guys behind him to go any faster because their legs and feet start bumping into the man in front of them. We were in last place, and as we had been in last place once before when we lost two of our guys, and had seen what happens, I really had a strong emotional desire not to lose. We were also being warned from the instructors that it pays to be a winner and that if we lost we would get unusual extra attention for losing. From the front, I was trying to motivate everyone to put out so that we wouldn't lose. I was trying to pick up the pace, but every time I did, I could feel and hear the two new guys behind me pulling back and whining. We were starting to fall back more, and I knew from the growing warnings from the instructors that we were close to getting extra attention when we were still over a mile from the finish. Something came over me—the catalyst was a strong desire not to fail. This emotion led to a strong mental determination to pass other boat crews so that we would not be last. This manifested itself physically, as I started picking up the pace, almost literally dragging the two resisting, crying guys until we started passing other boat crews. I was almost running, leaning and driving forward to move us forward. We passed several boat crews and easily finished well before the last boat crew, which was really getting hammered all the way into the finish. When we finished, we were able to sit and rest with the other winners, which was a luxury. When the last boat crew came in, we picked up and started moving again. This was a defining moment in my life, and it was a turning point for our boat crew, because we never lost a race after that evolution.

We excelled to the point where we were always fighting for the first place spot in every race.

I had learned from this event to emotionally spark a fire in my mind and my body that would help me get through stressful and challenging situations. Our two new guys had built a strong character from that one evolution and would now help out more throughout the rest of the week and even motivate the rest of us on a few occasions. Although they still struggled when we had to move around in the boats, they never held us back again.

On the flip side, emotions, when not directed properly, can lead to a debilitating stress in the other aspects of our physical and mental states. An example would be posttraumatic stress disorder (PTSD), which can affect anyone, not just combat soldiers, police, or firefighters.

Stress is used not just in the initial training of warriors/peacemakers, but also in the training afterwards to develop, hone, and sharpen greater skills. You learn to direct stress into a useful form or it overwhelms you and carries you away into negative forms, such as PTSD.

In the spring of 2004, I was in a small town named Diwaniha, which was located south of Baghdad, where I was in charge of a group sent to protect state department personnel that were assisting the Iraqis in developing local government. It had been a peaceful city, and for a few weeks nothing unusual was happening. We would leave our compound and drive a short distance to the government buildings in the center of town. Occasionally we would make moves into the surrounding countryside and support the surrounding communities with funds for local projects, such as new wells, sanitation, health clinics, bridges, roads, schools, women's centers, local government centers, police buildings, tribal centers, TV, and radio. Some of these projects had never been seen before, like the women's centers, and Saddam had outlawed others, like the tribal centers. The tribal centers were my favorite places to go because I could see that these men held the key to making Iraq work.

It was amazing to see the process of democracy spread, and the state department personnel were in excellent form. They would talk about how this was a rare opportunity that they had all trained their entire careers for and were really putting it into action in a way that many never imagined could happen. I talked with several locals who were excited about what was happening as well, and I said on one occasion, while talking with a young local leader, that it was possible that they could conceivably have a democracy that could be an example for the rest of the world. That all changed in one horrible day.

The Fallujah bridge incident in Iraq in the early part of 2004—wherein insurgents ambushed a convoy of contractors and shot, burned, mutilated, and finally dragged them through the streets and hung them from a local bridge—would start a wave of violence that would sweep through most of Iraq. Several of the guys I had known and worked with over the years as a SEAL and recently as a contractor were killed on that day. Our peaceful city south of Baghdad turned violent soon after that day, and our compound began to be mortared and the perimeter walls and fence attacked at night with RPGs and small arms fire. Other compounds with security contractors, such as in Najaf, beat back several hundred attackers. Others would not be so lucky and would have to be abandoned. We were able to beat back the initial perimeter attacks with a firestorm of bullets from our walls and the roofs of the compound's buildings. After we repulsed these initial attacks over several nights, the perimeter attacks stopped.

Soldiers from the Dominican Republic guarded the perimeter of our compound and gate. They were brave young men led by a young colonel who had a real sense of the environment they were in and managed his troops effectively. They were a contingent of the Spanish peacekeeping force sent in to keep the peace in Diwaniha and the surrounding province. The Spanish had a much larger force, with armored vehicles and well-armed troops, but they rarely went out to patrol. The Dominican Republic's savvy young colonel and his even younger troops had patrolled the streets of the city in armored pickup trucks with sheet metal bolted in the open bed of the truck to provide some protection to the troops riding in the back. This is fine for a peacekeeping force, but when the insurgents decided not to be peaceful anymore, it was no longer a good idea. One night shortly after the Fallujah incident, one of their vehicle patrols had come under attack from hand grenades, which had wounded some of the men in the open back of one of their makeshift armored trucks, and they, like the Spanish, had not resumed their patrols after that.

On the night of the first attack on our perimeter, the Dominican Republic troops had held their ground and really opened up with an incredible amount of firepower, and for the next few nights thereafter, there were only small, probing attacks throughout the night. These smaller attacks were met with a concentrated amount of fire directed at that point, and these attacks were easily repulsed. They also cleared the hospital building next to our compound and established an excellent vantage point from the roof of the highest building in town, which overlooked the entire city. They manned this point twenty-four/seven, along with the gate of our compound and the perimeter.

Because we contractors were the only security force still moving in the city, we were able to establish from the locals (who were very helpful and were furious that these men were using their town to hit us) the locations where they were setting up their mortar launch tubes. They were powerless to stop them, as they would show up at night with guns and set up a perimeter and terrorize the locals as they mortared our compound. We were told how the insurgents caused the women and children to cry at night, and the men felt powerless to stop them. We were asked for weapons that they could use to stop the hoodlums themselves, but we told them we didn't have the authority to help arm them. Later that same night, around the time we would be mortared, we heard gunshots in the area where we had spoken to the locals. That night, we didn't receive mortar fire and never would again from that location. Seems the locals of that neighborhood had gotten hold of some weapons after all.

We were also able to establish from the angry locals that the local gas station owners were sympathizers and were allowing the insurgents to use their gas station as a staging point. Late one night, when the town was quiet and deserted, we came under RPG fire from this gas station, and up to this point we had been very selective in our return fire so that we didn't harm the locals with stray rounds. Now that we knew that the gas station was providing aid and sanctuary to the insurgents, and we had established lanes of fire to prevent local casualties, we really lit that area up. From one of our sandbagged positions on the roof of a building that we had built for a machine gun post, I spotted a figure fire an RPG from the gas station. I watched in dread as the rocket traveled to our compound, leaving a smoky, fire-red jet trail in its wake, to cause death and mayhem. Luckily, it fell short and exploded on our perimeter fence.

I had carried a machine gun my entire career as a Navy SEAL, and I began firing with a similar machine gun, the M240, on a roof of our compound, looking out at the gas station. I put all my prior knowledge to use now, as I directed a heavy stream of red-hot tracer fire accurately all over the gas station area more than a thousand meters away; I knew that even if an explosion occurred, it would not cause collateral damage to the locals. I fired a continuous stream for almost a full minute until the barrel started glowing red and smoking. I could see the rounds impacting into the metal storage tanks of the gas station from the sparks my rounds were causing, and the red-hot tracer rounds will normally set fuel on fire. I knew I was causing damage and sending a strong message to the owners and whoever had fired the RPG. Fortunately for the owners of the gas station, tonight was not the night for the complete destruction of their facility.

We went back the next day with a team and surveyed the damage to the gas station, which was extensive, but the station remained operational. A high brick wall and large empty fuel tanks had shielded and protected the main tanks filled with fuel. The sparks from the rounds impacting and penetrating the metal were from the large, empty fuel tanks, and they had sustained a lot of damage from impacting rounds. As we surveyed the damage, I saw a new angle between some of the tanks that I could shoot through and hit the live fuel tanks if we ever were attacked from this location again.

Some of the management came out and started complaining about the damage. Neither of us understood the other's language, but I gestured to them that when rockets and gunfire came from their gas station, it would be met by return fire. I also gestured and made explosions. Then we got in our vehicles and left the area. Interestingly, we never received any kind of fire from that area again. In fact, we never received RPG or small arms fire at our compound again from any part of town during the nights to follow.

The mortar fire was a different story, though, as we continued to get mortars fired at our compound, which especially terrorized our Kellogg Brown and Root (KBR) contract cooks and administrative personnel. They, like many other contract workers, felt they had not signed on to come into what was turning into an intense combat zone, even though this was implied in their contracts and was the reason they were making far more than what their job descriptions entailed. When things were peaceful, it seemed like easy money to them, but now that the threat was real, they were ready to shut down the show and leave. It was the same throughout Iraq. Even some of the contractors I was working with were rejecting their jobs.

Fear and stress will cloud your thinking if you allow it to, and I was seeing a lot of it beginning to unfold. The emotion of fear is a very powerful one and can become rampantly contagious. Men will do things that they later regret, but these emotions are common in combat, if not directed properly. I had fortunately learned through extensive training and self-discipline how to direct these emotions so that they did not cloud my judgment and intuitional abilities. Among the contractor contingent that I was in charge of were former Chilean army troops. These were very focused, dependable men, some of whom had combat experience themselves. They were part of our static, or fixed, security and had been resourceful in building defenses and fighting positions on several of the rooftops in our compound and the government building in town. Not one of these men backed down from a fight, and they were always ready to help or position themselves to improve our overall security at our compound and the government building in town we traveled to on a daily basis.

Many of the guys on my team knew about my intuitional abilities, as I had proven them over a period of time and had begun to tell some of the guys I worked with how I was using them to help keep us safe. One particular day, I told the team that I had a feeling that something was happening in town and that we needed to be turned on and ready for action that day more than usual. This really got their attention, and as we started out that day, we were all extra alert. The entire time we were at the government building, I was having that nagging feeling increase in me that something was afoot. I made rounds of all of our positions in the government building, the rooftop, and outer perimeter, making sure everyone was alert and seeing if there was something else we could do to improve our positions. I talked with the local police that helped protect the provincial government building we were in, because sometimes they had information about possible attacks. They had heard nothing today, though. It was Friday, the Muslim world's equivalent to the Christian world's Sunday and Judaism's Saturday, so things were slow, as people were enjoying a relaxed day at home.

The State Department personnel finished up at the office early, and we started back in our two-vehicle convoy. Our lead car with the principals, or people we were protecting, were in an armored car, and the follow vehicle was unarmored, or "a soft skin." In the early days of Iraq, an armored vehicle was like gold and not a lot of them were available. We made the best of the follow SUV being a soft skin by turning it into a gun truck with a heavy automatic weapon in the back, shoulder fired automatic weapon on the passenger side, and two passengers with AK-47s on either side behind the driver.

We left the government administrative compound, and right away the driver of the vehicle I was in picked up speed at an unusually fast pace. This was good in a way, as we didn't normally go this fast because the streets were usually busy, but today was a slow day because of the holy day, and the streets were deserted. I had a quick thought that the streets seemed unusually deserted. Our speed was a trade-off in another way because reaction times would be less because of the high rate of speed, causing less maneuverability.

As I've said, fear can make your decision capability and reaction time decrease, and rather than making the guys more alert, as I felt my insight to them might have, some of them were visibly stressed in a negative way. The driver of the armored vehicle I was in with the principals was one of them. We were coming up on a corner where we had an option of taking a left and going over a bridge to vary our route or to round the rapidly approaching corner and take the fastest way to our compound. I had been feeling that something was up and at that moment I knew that just around the corner was an ambush waiting for us. I looked at the driver to tell him to take the alternate route, but I could see that he was in fear mode and had tunnel vision. I had worked with this guy enough over the past several weeks to know that he was not capable of quick changes or suggestions when he was in this mode.

Unfortunately, in the contracting world in the early days of the war, there were not enough highly skilled people available and properly screened to do high-threat work, and contracting companies would hire just about anybody that could point and shoot a weapon accurately. I had already tried to get a couple of guys replaced but was told by my company that I would have to make do with what I had.

Just before we rounded the corner, my only hope was that our unusually high rate of speed would give us an edge. I started to lift my radio to my mouth in anticipation of calling out to the follow vehicle about the ambush I felt was right around the corner. As we flew around the corner at breakneck speed, I saw a balaclava-clad man running across the street with an AK-47. He had been at a vantage point that he had taken up to watch for our approach. Our high speed had surprised him and he was dashing toward two more balaclava clad men who were raising their weapons to shoot at us but could not get a shot off because their point guy was between us and them. I quickly took it all in and instantly called out "ambush right, ambush right" and the already alert and ready follow vehicle rounded the corner right behind us and immediately opened up on the ambush. The ambush never got a shot off as we rocketed past and rounded the next corner.

Up to that point, we had never had an attack on our vehicles, and because it was a holy day, no one was outside, and the insurgents were able to set up unseen. We had surprised them instead of the other way around. My intuition had given us an edge, and we would live to see another day. After we surprised them, rather than the other way around, they would never try to ambush us again. This was another part of the process that I feel developed me to the point where my intuition gave me an almost preternatural ability to sense danger. Intuitional ability is like a muscle: the more you are aware of it, exercise it, and utilize it, the stronger and more accurate it gets.

Stress and being overly focused on one specific event limits your intuitional ability. I've learned to relax and go into the relaxation landmark of my mind more when stressful situations arise. It is not easy, and you want to fall back on what you know, even if you are aware that does not always serve you well. Higher states of consciousness are always just below our everyday hectic world and can be tapped, if trained properly through discipline and awareness of the different states of mind. They can be tapped even in life-or-death situations.

Emotions can be great catalysts for positive inherent capabilities that we all possess, or they can turn us toward negative stress-related problems. Understanding our emotional states can bring us great joy or great sorrow.

I remember days in Iraq when I was exhausted from staying up late fighting the insurgents and then the next day moving our principals around the province. I would get up early in the morning and sit outside before we began our day. I would think how stressful and dangerous our lives were, and then I quickly became aware how these thoughts and emotions were beginning to affect me negatively.

I decided to turn my thoughts from that point on to more

positive things, like how we were making a difference in the lives of the people in the surrounding community or anything of a positive nature. I would listen to the morning chorus of the birds singing and see the sun rising over the horizon, bringing its warmth and light, and I would think, "It's going to be a good day," and I would go out with a peaceful state of mind and start my day. The chaotic world of war would fall away, and my mind would become clear and focused.

Stressful situations were going to arise during the days to follow, but I would be able to handle them from a mind that was not debilitated by negative stress. If needed, I would now connect with the point in the morning where I had been at peace (my internal landmark). Being able to focus like a laser beam on events in combat with an unclouded mind was essential to survival, and by harnessing the emotional body in a positive way and using the stress that would occur in a focused and productive way, I would increase the chance of survival for the people I protected and the teams I worked with. I would develop these positive emotional habits in one of the most stressful environments known to man—armed combat. The learning curve in combat is high, and finding a way to deal with stress is one of the most important aspects in maintaining your ability to function during and after combat.

So not only must the physical and mental aspects of a warrior be honed, but also the emotional. When one of these aspects is lessened or disregarded, then the whole suffers. I would soon learn to hone another aspect of our natures that few realize exists and fewer still recognize for what it is: by far the most effective tool a warrior/peacekeeper could ever utilize.

"YOU CANNOT TEACH A MAN ANYTHING; YOU CAN ONLY HELP HIM FIND IT WITHIN HIMSELF."

◊ *Galileo Galilei* ◊

Chapter 4

TAPPING INTO THE HIGHER SELF

I have found that we have separate parts of ourselves that make a whole self, that make us wholly functional beings with the potential for vastly higher states of experience. I've alluded to these higher potentials throughout my story, and I will relate more experiences throughout this book. These separate parts that make us whole are the mental, physical, emotional, and spiritual states. When understood as separate parts of the whole, the physical, mental, and emotional bodies can be effectively utilized for tapping into the higher self.

When I speak of "the higher self," it could mean spiritual self to you or whatever term you use to account for your greater potential that is beyond our three-dimensional world. When I speak of spirituality, I am not referring to any particular religion or way of life. Although religions can be guides to helping humanity find our spiritual or higher selves, and I have found beauty and thought-provoking inspiration from all of the world's religions, I have also found that taking individual responsibility for developing my higher self has given me a greater understanding of myself as a "spiritual being having a human experience," rather than a "human having a spiritual experience."

As a collective, humanity is evolving from emotionally-oriented, individual societal groups into a mind-oriented, wholly integrated group. We are becoming interdependent politically, economically, culturally, etc., and if one country or group decides to act independently, in a negative or positive way, it is increasingly affecting the entire world. Just as our physical bodies depend on our interdependent respiratory, circulatory, skeletal, nervous, and digestive systems to operate smoothly, our society depends on the many different systems of all the different countries and groups of the world. We can no longer ignore any culture or disallow any one group or individual from achieving the highest good that they can, and it is in the best interests of the entire body collective that we all take responsibility, not just for our own growth, but for the collective as well. If one part of the collective is not achieving an understanding of its highest self or greatest good, it will bring down the rest of the body collective, or humanity.

We should look at the different aspects of ourselves and understand each of these aspects as having to be developed evenly to balance ourselves as a whole. Each person develops differently, and if one aspect of us is neglected, then it reduces our overall effectiveness and development. For instance, suppose a political leader had developed his mind to a high degree and gave exceptional speeches that motivated and inspired millions, but had not developed his emotional side. This political leader could be prone to wild mood swings, which would cloud his highly developed mind and cause irrational decisions. This undeveloped part of the political leader's emotional decisions in turn would likely cause these same inspired millions to suffer and wonder at how such a seemingly great leader could cause such hardships after having inspired them before.

I have traveled over much of the world and can say that in all my travels, even to some of the most violent places on earth, I have not found a group of people that were not friendly and willing to treat others with respect and dignity if those others forwarded the same intention. This does not mean that my kindness should be mistaken for weakness, but that I am secure and confident enough in my own abilities and the goodwill of others, until proven otherwise, that I can extend myself when the situation permits.

Now to return to the town of Diwaniha, in which we were being mortared consistently almost every night for a couple of weeks in our compound. During the day, we would analyze the trajectory of the blast patterns on the walls of the buildings and blast holes in the ground to determine where the mortar tubes were being set up during the night to fire into our compound. We would then go out into the neighborhoods to the likely locations, fully armed, looking for the spots they had fired from. As we came into the different neighborhoods, the local populace would tell us of the terror they were going through at night. They gave us any information we needed and were very frustrated. These people were most generous when we arrived and would offer to have us in for tea; they were some of the most cordial people I have come across anywhere. I am certain that some of the people that I made friends with would still offer kindness if I were to go back there someday in the future when Iraq is a settled place. Some of the people even told us, "If you come back to our village twenty years from now, we will remember you and consider you our friends and invite you into our homes." Throughout my travels in the Middle East, I have found that 90 percent of the people are this friendly, and the 10 percent who are violent control the rest of the people through force, and thus, unfortunately, are the ones who are usually running the countries. I believe they are capable of this because the people in the Middle East are so gentle as a whole.

The insurgents were, on average, young males between the ages of seventeen and twenty-one, many of whom were known to be drug users. When these hoodlums (I call them that because the locals did) set up their tubes at night, they would show up with a group armed with AKs and terrorize the neighborhoods they were setting up in, shoot a few mortars at us, and then take off. They were growing increasingly emboldened and taking more time to set up and fire more rounds. They had found a couple of neighborhoods where they could intimidate the locals and were getting the angles down for their fire.

The mortar rounds had been ineffective at first, but they were getting increasingly more accurate, and instead of dropping one to three rounds on us like before, they were dropping six to nine, and getting more rounds into our compound. It was only a matter of time before the knuckleheads that were mortaring us figured out how to properly aim their tubes and started hitting us with more effective fire, so we felt we needed to take some action soon because no one else was up to the task or felt the need to get involved. The local police were either part of the problem or were wary of getting involved for fear of retribution from the hoodlums; the U.S. military deferred to the Spanish, who were in charge of our province. The Spanish had tried to patrol the town like the Dominican Republic troops, but felt it was too dangerous, so they no longer patrolled the town at night.

Over a period of time, we located a few spots that the insurgents had found which afforded them a good trajectory into our compound for their mortar fire. We were putting all the pieces together to put an end to the insurgents' deadly nightly game.

From the vantage point of the hospital next to our building, we set up some of our contractors during the night to spot where the flashes (from the mortars leaving their mortar tubes) were coming from.

We as contractors were a varied group, mostly from several different military units, and a couple of us had come up with the plan to counter battery the mortar teams that were harassing us every night. We had a small contingent of U.S. military assigned to a motor vehicle repair unit that was temporarily stationed in our compound. They had an MK19 automatic grenade launcher on one of their vehicles that they let us borrow. Unfortunately, they were not allowed to be out and help us fight when we were being attacked, but were instead ordered to remain inside the safety of the cement buildings that made up our compound. We came up with a plan to use the MK19 from the roof of one of our buildings to launch grenades back at the mortars. The MK19 could be vehicle mounted or used with a tripod, like a mortar, and could be adjusted to accurately put rounds down range. Our plan was to fire rounds into the areas from which the mortars were launched. We had already paced off and calculated the many different known locations throughout town, and we would use the roof of the hospital to spot and adjust our fire to these locations. We would also use the guys on the roof of the hospital to radio us so that we could walk our rounds in, adjusting our fire if we were not on target.

When we first started to fire back at them, our rounds had landed close to them, and through our spotters on the hospital roof, we started to walk our rounds into the best position from which to fire at the insurgents. We thought our last three round volleys had made it into their location because we didn't receive more than the initial three rounds from them, instead of the eight or nine we had been receiving.

We went back the next day to survey the location, but found our last three rounds had impacted on a roof just in front of the hoodlums' location and probably gave them a good scare, but didn't cause them any damage.

We continued our vigilance on the roofs, but had no attacks for several nights. We were beginning to believe that we had scared them off for good. Normally, they would mortar us between ten p.m. and two a.m., so we would stay on the roofs during that time frame and long after, ready to strike back. It was after two a.m. on the fourth night, after we had counter battered them, and we felt they weren't going to hit us again, so I called the guys off their position from the roofs so they could get some rest.

I had been washing and drying my clothes in a makeshift laundry room in a field in between buildings in our compound. I went to gather up my clothes and was taking them out of the dryer and folding them when rounds started leaving mortar tubes. Up to this point, they had used just one tube, but now I could hear two being used, rounds thumping out of tubes in rapid succession. I grabbed my radio and called the guys who had left the hospital roof to see if they were on the ground in the compound or still in the hospital making their way down from the rooftop. When I called them, I could hear them running and breathing heavy as they answered, saying they were halfway to our compound and in the open, trying to make it to the buildings. Just then, rounds started impacting inside our compound. I yelled over the radio for them to find cover where they were and lay low. The ground shook, and I could tell by the sound that the rounds were hitting the vehicles that the Dominican Republic army had staged around the other side of the building from where I was in the laundry room. In quick succession, the rounds started working around the building and were heading toward the plywood structure I was in. I hit the floor, and through a crack in the door, I could look out and see the mortar rounds walking their way to my location. The impact of the rounds, their ground shuddering explosions in close proximity to my location, and the sound of shrapnel thudding into the plywood of the building I was in were growing louder as the rounds quickly worked their way toward my fragile sanctuary. I could hear the shrapnel starting to splinter the plywood, and I knew the next couple of rounds would probably land close enough to send shrapnel through the plywood and into my body. I tried to make my self as flat as possible and scooted under a folding table to give me a little more protection in case a round landed on top of the plywood structure I was in. I started praying fervently and imagined an impenetrable dome over the building I was in. Suddenly the rounds stopped. I thanked God and quickly called the guys who had been caught in the open. They said they were fine and had gotten small themselves, down by a wall on the other side of the compound. The damage to several of the vehicles was extensive, but no one was hurt. We figured they had brought in some more experienced guys and had lookouts in the hospital who had informed them when our lookouts had come down.

We had another surprise for them, though. We had also determined that within an hour after they mortared us, they would load up their car and fly down the long stretch of road across from the gas station area they were mortaring us from. It was the same car and time frame every time after we were mortared. As no cars at all would be on the roads from around nine p.m. until early light, we easily determined it was our hoodlum gang. We waited with our automatic weapons, and when the car came into firing range in an intersection several hundred meters across from our outpost, we lit their car up. The car was completely disabled in the intersection, and we continued to fire shots at it if we saw any movement. We couldn't tell if we had hit anyone because of the distance and because there were no streetlights working in that area. The distance was far enough away from the roof of the hospital where we had restationed our guys that they couldn't tell if anyone was still in the vehicle or not. It was late and we all had to work in the morning, so we asked the Dominican Republic guards to shoot at anyone trying to get into that vehicle. The next morning, the vehicle was gone, and when we asked the guards what had happened, they said that several men had shown up just before dawn and had towed the vehicle away. We asked why they hadn't fired, and they said they couldn't without authorization and unless they were being fired at.

We found that this was the mentality among all the military units, regardless of nationality. We were at war, and instead of taking the fight to the enemy, everyone was trying to conduct a police action. Unconventional forces were conducting unconventional warfare against us all across Iraq, and we were trying to combat it with conventional forces, which was wrong to begin with. These conventional forces were not even conducting conventional warfare, which would have been wrong as well, but somewhat more effective than the police action they were being forced to conduct, which was beyond insane. This was an unconventional warrior's dream come true. I had trained for over two decades for this type of warfare, and if I had been on the other side, it would have been far more devastating. Now, instead of being the hunter, I was the fox, but I still had some sharp teeth, and I knew the game these dogs were playing and knew it well.

The next night, we knew it would be game on, and we really needed to take it to them or they would start taking us out of the compound in body bags. The hoodlums had very nearly accomplished that.

We decided to have a trick worked out to try and fool whoever was watching our movements in the hospital. We knew the hospital staff was negative toward us, as we had gone over to the hospital with one of the State Department personnel after the Dominican Republic personnel had gone into the building to occupy the roof. We had gone in to allay their concerns, and an angry demonstration had mysteriously materialized the moment after we had entered the building. In the Middle East, there are still many people ruled by emotions, and they can be very easily spun up into an angry and violent mob by even the slightest perceived or manipulated perception of wrong against them. Within minutes of our arrival, the demonstration outside of our conference was being turned into one of these angry mobs, and I knew from experience you don't stick around on these occasions. The atmosphere in the room with the doctors and hospital leadership was not a positive one either; some of the men who had entered the room were becoming very animated. I kept motioning to the State Department personnel that we needed to go, as I was in communication with the guys who were watching the mob scene growing outside the hospital. They were near where we were and would cut off our only escape route if they entered the building. I finally politely interrupted after getting no response from repeated high signs; it was time to go and go right now. We collapsed our security as we headed out the back of the building and passed by the glass doors where we could hear the angry mob sounds and see the people as they were starting to press against the doors we had secured. After this incident, we felt the hospital staff was relaying our movements to the local terrorist gang, so to counter this, we came up with a ruse to fool them. During our nightly watch movements on and off the roof of the hospital, we had previously used the hospital's elevators to access the roof. We would now counter their spy network by sending a relief team up the outside steps in back of the building instead of through the building to the elevators. Our plan was that the team would come down the elevators in the hospital around the time we usually ended the watch on the roof. We figured the hospital spy would notify the terrorists that we no longer had anyone on the roof to counter their mortaring of our compound. We would see if they took the bait.

The MK19 team was ready, but we had a problem. After a couple of weeks of playing cat and mouse with their mortar team, we were down to just nine rounds left, or three volleys. We had also been on a learning curve, but had gotten our timing and accuracy quickly down with the rounds going out, and the coordination with spotters on the roof was quicker and more accurate as well. They had caught us off guard last time, but we would be ready this time. I felt that they would be counting on catching us off guard again, and, sure enough, when our decoy team came down from the roof through the inside elevator after they were relieved by the other team going up the outside steps, the insurgents began mortaring.

We had this crazy game of running down the steps from the roof of the main building where we would watch for an attack on our perimeter. If we hadn't held a vigil on the perimeter, we could have easily been overrun because there were several spots on the perimeter fencing that were weak. As the hospital roof team called rounds out, the guys who were not in hardened sandbag locations with sandbagged roofs would run down the stairs to the safety of the concrete building's lower floors. We were being mortared by 60mm rounds, which were the approximate equivalent of five hand grenades bundled together. They would cause external shrapnel damage to a concrete building or sandbagged position, but you could easily survive if inside. If you were outside, then you could be hit by shrapnel, which could cause blood loss from the many razorblade-like shrapnel cuts to the skin. If you were closer to the blast, deeper cuts could sever arteries and veins. If directly next to the blast, you could have enough internal trauma from the blast wave to cause immediate death.

You may recall that I had mentioned that the Army maintenance group had been ordered to stay indoors during shelling. Unfortunately, they tried to play the game we were by running up to the roof after the shells dropped to survey the damage. They were on another building and we didn't have communication with them, and to my knowledge they had never been on the roof before. A couple of their personnel ran to the roof to get a look just as two rounds struck their rooftop building. I had been below the roof of our building and had heard the rounds coming down on the other side of our compound and outside our perimeter. I had a practiced ear after several weeks of being mortared and could tell where the rounds were coming from, where they would approximately land, and how long I had before they started impacting. I had run back to our roof just as a volley of rounds worked across the perimeter fence and landed on top of a building several hundred meters across from us. The moment it went off, I knew someone had been hit, even though it was pitch-black and we could not hear any other sound through all the explosions. I made a comment to the guys around me that someone got hurt with that one, but in the heat of the battle our attention was immediately drawn back to the need to get rounds back out from our side.

Our guys on the hospital roof had called out the location of the mortar tubes, and we were sending our own rounds out before the mortar rounds even landed in our compound. Our mortar team was by far the bravest in our group. They were on an isolated part of the roof that was above the rest of the roof and had to climb a tall wooden ladder to reach their perch. While they had built a small sandbagged shelter with a sandbagged protective roof, the MK19 itself was out in the open in front of their position, and if a round landed squarely on their position, they would have been blown off in pieces. While we ran down to the protection below or ducked down into well-fortified bunkers, they stayed on their isolated perch, sending rounds back out to the hoodlums. Our first volley had landed close, and we quickly adjusted and sent out the next volley, leaving us with just one volley left. Everyone in our group held their breath as we waited for the roof team to call out where the rounds were impacting. We could hear more mortars going out, so the hoodlums felt confident in their new location and were not going to run as they had on previous nights when we returned fire. They were mortaring us from a location where they had never been before, and it must have been a good one. They may not have even heard or seen our first volley, as it landed just as they were sending out their second volley. We ran down the stairs again, and as we heard the rounds impacting in a different area of the compound, we ran back up. I could see the rounds coming down into a courtyard area in the center of our compound and saw a round land on a sandbagged area on another roof used by the Dominican Republic personnel. I didn't have the feeling that someone was hit, like I had on the first volley, even though it was an obvious hit on a sandbagged position. We learned later that several of the sandbags had been blown off the position, but the guys inside were unhurt.

We returned our focus to finishing this fight with a vengeance, and I radioed to the roof team to find out where our last volley had landed. They replied that we were just short and that one of our rounds had been on target; a small adjustment would put us on target. I was surprised by this and had my doubts, but I told our counter battery team to make the quick adjustment and send only one round. It was on target! We quickly sent out our remaining two rounds and were told they were on target as well. As I listened to the distant explosions from our rounds, I got the same feeling that I had had when I felt someone was being hurt on a rooftop in our compound. I told our group, "We finally got them."

It became very silent after all the explosions and we got a report that someone was injured in the compound and we sent our 18 Delta medical corpsman to help out. Sure enough, on the building where I had said someone was hurt, one of the Army personnel had been injured when he put one foot on the roof just as a mortar round had gone off. He had been coming out of a covered doorway and the only thing that was hit was his exposed leg. The rest of his body was unhurt and luckily the two guys running up behind him had not yet made it out onto the open roof. Fortunately, the soldier's wounds were stabilized, and he was medevaced by a helo at first light, just a couple of hours later.

We had fired our last round from the MK19 and now we would lose that weapon as well because the army unit was ordered to evacuate immediately. By the time we all got up and had breakfast, they were all gone.

Later that day, we loaded up and went out to survey the damage we had possibly caused to the hoodlums. We navigated our way through a neighborhood on the other side of the street from the hospital where the mortar rounds had come from and where we had returned fire. When we came to the approximate location, we were greeted by a throng of people that came out of their homes and guided us to the location where the hoodlums had set up their mortars. We could see the indentation in the ground where two base plates had hammered into the ground from the shock of the rounds thumping out of the mortar tubes after the propellant had ignited. You could see where three 40mm grenades had fallen and exploded around and between the two mortar tubes. The locals from the neighborhood we were in excitedly shared with us how all of the mortar teams had been hurt and had gone to the hospital.

I learned through the local intelligence network that we had developed, that the terrorists said, "The American contractors have a grenade hunting machine that has grenades that find us and hurt us." This was the name they gave our MK19, which they thought had a homing device capability set just for them. We all had a good laugh when we heard this; it was partially a laugh of amusement and partially of stress relief.

For the rest of the time that I was in charge at the site in Diwaniha after we put the mortar teams in the hospital, we were never attacked again in any way. We had foiled all of their attacks and not one of the contractor teams I was in charge of, or any of the people we were tasked with keeping safe, had suffered so much as a scratch.

The terrorists had not been so lucky, but amazingly, we had only given them a good beating and not one of them was killed by our return fire and counter ambushes.

My intuition had played a big part in keeping us safe over the last several weeks by alerting me to impending attacks. I had known when it was safe to move our group around town so that we could track down the hoodlums, triangulate their mortar positions, and eventually beat them at their own game. I would continue to develop this natural inherent ability that all of us have within us but few of us believe in or believe we can develop. Over the next several years, I would save countless teammates and people we were in charge of keeping safe from danger by using intuition. I would also develop other powerful skills inherent in all humans, but which few recognize and many dismiss as impossible.

"YOU MUST TRAIN YOUR INTUITION—YOU MUST TRUST THE SMALL VOICE INSIDE YOU, WHICH TELLS YOU EXACTLY WHAT TO SAY, WHAT TO DECIDE."

◊ *Ingrid Bergman* ◊

Chapter 5

HOW TO AWAKEN YOUR INTUITION

To awaken or increase your awareness, higher self, and intuition is a great challenge today. I believe that we have three areas that must first be disciplined before we can move to a point where intuition can develop successfully. The rewards for a disciplined approach to manifesting intuition are well worth the effort. As an intuitively aware being, you will have a direct connection to the formless stuff that makes up everything within the universe. You will be connected to your divine self through intuition and have the ability to manifest what you most focus your thoughts on. As your intuition develops, you will open many doors to the unseen worlds, and you will become a witness to the power of the science of spiritual knowledge. Science and spiritual knowledge have veered onto separate paths, but intuition brings them back together where they belong.

You must have the intense discipline of a warrior mind-set to initially develop your intuition. Through the three disciplines that

I will outline, a three keys system of meditation, and a three-step process of consistent practice, you will become intuitional or advance your current level of intuition. Throughout this book, I have given many examples of the development and use of intuition in my life and have said that this ability is inherently natural to all humanity. We will now look at the how-to of intuition.

The three disciplines we must initially master within ourselves are:

Instinctual urges that focus our attention toward comfort and gratification of the lower self. Strict self-gratification will keep you rooted in the basic level of human existence, and this level is usually based in fear. I am not saying that you cannot gratify your senses—only that complete focus on our basic desires is what holds us back. This level of base instinctual urges will distract you from seeking a connection to the next level of advancement, which is the intellect.

Intellectual mind chatter stems from a mind that controls who and what you are. You are not your mind but something much greater. Until your higher self is in charge of your thoughts, you will be like a ship adrift at sea that goes where your random thoughts take you. A disciplined mind can be used to focus thoughts to the intention of the higher self. By learning to focus our thoughts, we begin to manifest our desires in life. As we become more aware of our ability to manifest our world through our disciplined intellect, we will naturally advance to the intuitional level.

The more aware you become of your intuition abilities in the beginning, the more you will have to discipline yourself and stay grounded and balanced with the rational world. Becoming consciously intuitional is not the end of the game, because at this point in our advancement, we need to stay connected with the rational world, or our spiritual knowledge will become too abstract for the material or scientific world and will never manifest itself.

If we develop the discipline that I have outlined above, we will open the door to our intuitional abilities, which is the next step in the advancement of the human race. We have mainly moved from the base level of consciousness or instinctual awareness to intellectual awareness, where the majority of humanity resides. Ultimately, we will continue from intellect to intuitional awareness as a human race.

To further understand what is needed for advancement to an intuitional ability, we need to first look toward Eastern philosophy and culture. To find one half of what we need to advance into an intuitional awareness, we need to have the Eastern mentality of focus on wisdom, mystical development, reflection, uniqueness, individuality, and meditation. In the West, where we find the other half of the equation for our abilities, the major focus is on acquiring knowledge, science, investigation, and memory training. Both methods are correct, but they are usually mutually exclusive. The West and East are apt to exclude each other's methods, but both in and of themselves are fundamentally correct. Each could supplement and complement the other, and therefore to practice both would best allow mankind to begin to manifest intuitional abilities.

We can liken the Eastern and Western hemispheres of the earth to the two hemispheres of the brain. The left hemisphere of the brain, or Western thought, processes information in a linear, sequential, logical manner, and with objective reasoning; it is local or physical in nature. When using the left brain, you process information piece by piece, like you would a math problem or science experiment.

The right hemisphere of the brain, or Eastern thought, is more visual and processes intuitively, holistically, randomly, and by subjective reasoning. The right brain is fluid and spontaneous and non-local in reality.

By bridging the objective, rational left hemisphere with the subjective, intuitive right hemisphere, we can create a humanity that has its feet firmly placed on the ground and at the same time be intuitive, inspired, and have the ability to change our world from one of war, conflict, and fear to one of peace, joy, and love. For one of the most inspirational stories you will find, and one that will give you excellent insight into the hemispheres of the brain and how they function, read brain researcher Jill Bolte Taylor's book *My Stroke of Insight*.

Once we have disciplined our instinctual urges and intellect, and have a grasp of how we need to bridge the gap between Western and Eastern thought, we can begin to seriously develop our own intuition.

I have found that there are three keys to effective meditation:

The first key in this process is to relax the body. I usually start at the bottom of my body and work my way up by alternately relaxing the feet, legs, groin area, back, torso, arms, hands, neck, face, and head. With your body relaxed, you will not be distracted.

The second key is controlling the breathing. Take long, deep, steady breaths through the nose that fill the lungs, pause, and then slowly release the breath through the nose or mouth.

The third key is focusing the mind on a single point. In the beginning, you can focus on the breath as a single focal point. If you notice the mind chatter come into your awareness, refocus on the breath again.

The first two keys are easy, and the third will be as well, but it will take a little more practice, as the ego will do anything it can to convince you that this is ridiculous, a waste of time, etc. This is where the work you did to master the first three disciplines comes in handy as you learn to transcend the mind chatter.

Now you are ready to focus on your intent, which is to develop your intuition. As you master your mind and turn it inward, pick a focal point in your body. I focus on the area between the eyes and slightly up and back within the middle of the brain. Without straining your eyes, imagine looking into the middle of your head to a point slightly above your eyes. This point is the pineal gland, and it is about the size of a pea. It is shaped like a pinecone, hence the name. This point is often called the third eye. The pineal is divided into two fine hemispheres and sits directly between both hemispheres of the brain, linking the two. The pineal gland is bioluminescent and sensitive to light, hence the name third eye. Most importantly, it is the connecting link between the physical and spiritual worlds and higher frequencies.

With a relaxed body, deep breathing, and focus on the third eye, you will open the doorway to the higher self, which in turn will link to all that is, or the divine intelligence. Your creative imagination will be activated, you will begin to visualize, and the thought energy of the mind will give life and direction to your visualization. Intuition is achieved through third eye development. I have found that over time I no longer need to go into a meditation to get insights from my third eye. When I get insights, I slow everything down and focus on my pineal gland, and that's when I usually get my creative insights to questions or have visualizations of future events. It is from this point that I send out the energy of love, change my physical environment, or visualize what I want to create or attract into my life.

Discipline, or staying focused and daily using and linking with the idea of using your intuition, is crucial in the beginning so that you create a habit. Develop the habit of connecting with your pineal/third eye on a daily basis for twenty to thirty minutes for twenty-one days to create a habit.

Numerology is the relationship between physical objects or living things. Numerological divination was popular among early mathematicians such as Pythagoras, but is no longer considered part of mathematics by modern scientists. In 325 AD, following the First Council of Nicaea, the spiritual significance of the "sacred" numbers was officially disapproved as a belief and classified as a civil violation if practiced.

The number that I used for linking with your pineal gland is three, which means communication/interaction. All three of the threes for linking with your pineal equal nine, which means highest level of change. The two in twenty-one days to a habit is balance, or yin, the feminine aspect, and the number one for yang, the masculine aspect. Everything is considered one or the other with a balancing aspect of the opposite. This book contains twenty-one chapters, which is a balance of masculine and feminine.

The scientific and spiritual knowledge link has been taken out of so many aspects of our lives. The scientific is masculine, and the spiritual knowledge is the feminine aspect. If we look to our brains, we have the masculine side of the brain that is the left hemisphere, and the feminine side that is the right side. The earth is divided into a masculine or Western half and the feminine, which is the Eastern half of the globe. Earth is considered the feminine aspect and the cosmos is the masculine aspect by many earth based indigenous American tribes. Our pineal gland links us to all these aspects, has a left and right hemisphere, and is centered within the hemispheres of the brain. The masters have taught us that everything we need to know is within us. That point is the pineal gland, and it will open the door to your intuition and connect you with your divine self, which is all-knowing.

"FIRST, BEGIN BETWEEN SELVES. SET A DEFINITE TIME, AND EACH AT THAT MOMENT PUT DOWN WHAT THE OTHER IS DOING. DO THIS FOR TWENTY DAYS. AND YE WILL FIND YE HAVE THE KEY TO TELEPATHY."

◊ *Edgar Cayce* ◊

(on developing telepathy)

Chapter 6

AN ADVANCED FORM OF COMMUNICATION

Another thing that I began to grasp early on in my career as a Navy SEAL was the ability I and others developed after we had worked together over a period of time: the ability to communicate wordlessly. This of course began as a need to be silent during our various training evolutions, which were, quite frankly, much tougher than the real combat missions that I would later participate in. I remember how we would go through the basics of hand and arm signals as we first began to work with a new group. We would practice these signals constantly through all of our training missions, whether it was on land during patrolling or live weapon room clearance during Close Quarter Combat (CQC), underwater during diving, or during parachute operations. We eventually began to not use them at all. A really in-tune group of operators will rarely talk or use hand and arm signals for long periods of time, but will perform multiple tasks that it would take hours of coordination for an untrained group of people to get as perfectly synchronized as even one of the simple tasks that these groups perform repeatedly. Things would change during our missions, as they always do, and a well-seasoned group would shift gears without missing a beat; oftentimes, it would be done wordlessly.

I have always been a big fan of science and the scientific process and had started reading all I could find on this subject early on in my career as a war fighter. I remember being fascinated as a kid in the early seventies by a show on TV called *The Sixth Sense*. On the show, a doctor, who is a college professor, and his assistant have an interest in the paranormal and study the psychic abilities in others. On one episode in particular, they studied the ability of one person to send telepathic thoughts to another. A friend and I tried some of the techniques they were using to send thoughts. One of the techniques we used was to focus on a single thought, like the color red or the number ten, then send that thought until the other person clearly got it; we had amazing success with this technique.

Since I embarked on my own scientific investigation of the expanded consciousness that I was experiencing, I have found that scientists from every scientific discipline were pushing the frontiers of their respective science. *The Field* and *The Intention Experiment* by Lynn McTaggart are an excellent example of a couple of books out of hundreds that I've read over the years, which delve into the many different sciences and scientists that are undertaking these amazing studies. The pioneering scientists described in these books are pushing the limits of our understanding of our world. Like other scientific pioneers before them, such as Galileo, they are often criticized and discounted by scientific, religious, or political institutions still stuck in outdated information and dogma. As a collective, humanity is constantly evolving, but many are afraid of change or of losing their power and control. They will do anything to hold on to their control rather than make the effort to accept the inevitable progression of humanity. I've found that the truth of any matter has a way of ultimately prevailing, and the information that is being presented by these brave warriors in the scientific community will ultimately benefit mankind in tremendous ways.

As I observed the phenomenon of nonverbal or visual communication transpiring throughout my interactions with others throughout my life, I began to try and consciously communicate my intention to others telepathically. I found again that the more relaxed I was when I sent the thoughts, the more likely they would be received. I remember times when we would patrol to targets for combat training that would take many days and nights to get to. After several hours of walking with gear on, you start to move into a rhythm with the group as you move over the varying landscape while trying to be as silent as possible. Just being in the wilderness or remote areas brings about a rhythm with the environment as you begin to intuitively know how the landscape will unfold. After a while, the group would begin to become one, not just in movement, but in thought as well. I could tell what the point man was silently discussing or motioning to the team leader without even hearing or seeing their interactions. The word would be whispered back down the group to the rest of us after a decision was made, but over time this was not even necessary as everyone just started to intuitively know what we were doing.

Even before caller identification came out, I would often know who was calling before I answered the phone. If you have a close connection with someone, you are aware of this, as the moment you think of someone, he or she will show up or call.

I would learn through teamwork how to become intuitive and aware of others' thoughts, because of a need to be silent. It was as if we were taking one thing away and heightening our other senses to the point where we were becoming extrasensory or beyond the accepted range of senses. Some of the guys I worked with during my career would actually know what the other forces that were out trying to hunt us down were thinking.

On one occasion, a force that was highly trained to track down special operations forces was out hunting us during a training mission and our point man stopped our patrol for no apparent reason and had us move at a run in the opposite direction. For a patrol to do an about-face and run is highly unusual, but we trusted our point man and ran in the other direction as quietly as possible. None of us had heard or seen a thing; we just trusted him and did it. The next night, we again were stopped in midstride by this same point man and turned around and quickly set up an ambush at his direction. Again, none of us had seen or heard anything, and we never saw anyone. The next day, we were told at a debriefing that never had the force that was hunting us encountered a group that they did not eventually ambush. We had not only foiled them, but they had said that we had almost walked into their ambush the first night when we mysteriously disappeared. The second night they said that they had heard us and as they were patrolling to our position, they stopped just before our ambush, but turned around after not hearing us anymore. I asked our point man later how he had done it, and he said he would tell me because he knew I would understand and had an open mind and that he had "heard" their thoughts, but had not physically heard them.

I have been a student of military history for a long time, and studying the American Civil War gave me the idea that Generals Jackson and Lee of the Confederate Army were both reading the thoughts of the opposing army, in my opinion. When questioned after periods of silence and obvious meditation as to what they were thinking, they would say that they were trying to assess the opposing generals' or armies' thoughts and intentions. They were uncanny in their ability to attack, maneuver, feint, and disappear just at the right time and often with a smaller force. General Jackson would ride close to the front lines and stare in the direction of the fighting as if trying to intuit the direction of fighting and where the weak points were. I feel that many great generals throughout time have been able to connect with this intuitive side of themselves and read the thoughts and intentions of their opponents.

One of the greatest obstacles to developing these gifts that are inherent in all of us is the doubt over their existence and our ability to develop them. I was fortunate to have examples from others who knew they had the ability to read others, and I would eventually develop the ability to not only read others' thoughts, but also learn how to mask my thoughts so that I did not telegraph them. I would teach these skills to others later when I was running the hand-to-hand course. Teamwork and sharing information is crucial to not only a team's success, but also to a team's development.

I remember throughout my career as a SEAL and high risk security contractor that some of my colleagues would find a particularly beneficial way of doing our jobs and keep it selfishly to themselves in the belief that they would excel and have a better chance for recognition as a high achiever and therefore a better chance at advancement or job security.

This goes against the intention and spirit of teamwork, because as an individual excels at a particular task and shares it, the whole benefits, and if the collective group learns how to effectively reproduce this ability, then the group can reach an even higher level of achievement and foster more creative achievement. Individuals who selfishly withhold from a group that depends on group participation do not do well. That is why our SEAL training stressed group participation so that many examples are experienced to reinforce the value of a group working together.

For instance, I was strong at paddling and would often take up the toughest position in the front of the IBS during Hell Week and set the example by using strong, deep strokes and calling out the cadence; I would also help motivate the other guys by urging them to do the same. This took extra initiative and energy, but the alternative was falling behind and getting hammered by the instructors. So I could have just sat in the middle of the boat and selfishly dipped my paddle in the water and let it drift back in time with the other paddles to conserve my individual energy, or I could add to the collective and we could all work hard together and offer what we could to the group. By working together, we avoided extra attention, which would have been more debilitating and costly in the long run. So we learned, sometimes the hard way, that it pays to be a winner and work together to achieve a level that would not have been possible with a group of individuals.

Later, as instructors, we would watch carefully for individuals who would not work with the group and who tried to slack off and let the rest of the group carry their load. These sly individuals, when caught, would really get some heat. Sometimes carrying the load for the others would cause an injury, but if a person was weak in one area but expended extra energy in other areas to make up for it, it would balance out the team. I remember one Hell Week in which an officer of a boat crew was starting to limp and fall behind. We had been watching him throughout the preceding weeks up to and including Hell Week, and he had been an inspiration and motivation for his boat crew and an excellent example for his class. Normally, we would have singled him out, but we were allowing his boat crew to actually help him as he had helped others in many ways up to this point. He was really starting to fall behind on this particular evolution, which was a four-mile timed run as a boat crew rather than as an individual. We were ready to pull him out, because his limp was getting so bad, which would have resulted in him having to repeat Hell Week and start with a new class. The rest of the students in his boat crew would gather around him and wrap their arms around his waist and help to carry his weight, which was helping. Normally, we would not allow this much help, but we had seen him contribute to such a high level that we knew he would make up for it in another area. We were also running a fine line between a more debilitating injury and an injury that could be healed in a few weeks before the next class started up.

There comes a time when the highest self of all becomes involved. I had the idea that we could pull him and do an on-the-spot medical analysis while the boat crew finished the race. If he weren't severely injured, we would put him back in close to the finish. This would be the last time the class had a long run where his boat crew would not be able to help him more. Also, if he lasted a few more hours, he would be rolled forward rather than back if his injury worsened.

The corpsman who was to do the analysis had the same idea that I did. We had worked together at SEAL Team Six, and we both had the same thought without even speaking to each other. This was a trait that others and I would develop, understand, and accept over the years, and that I would eventually come to recognize as telepathy. He was an expert at his job, and if there was a chance the officer could go on, then he would be able to determine it. If we had waited until the end of the race, then it was clear to us that the officer would be broken and not be able to continue. One of the other instructors working with us was also a guy that I had worked with extensively in the teams, and he knew what we were up to by a quick glance at the situation. Almost all of the groups that I would work with and create a professional rapport with over many years as an operator and security contractor would have this ability to read a situation or people quickly without words being spoken.

The ability to telepathically communicate developed within me by happenstance over time while I was in the SEAL teams. It happened mainly with people I worked with through a desire and need to anticipate my teammates' movements while moving silently. Initially, I realized that through eye contact and reading body language I was able to anticipate what others would do to a certain degree. When I could not visibly see my teammates on military maneuvers, I would listen for their movements, but I found myself beginning to accurately anticipate movements without the five senses we are used to using. When I first realized I was intuitively anticipating others' movements, I wondered why and was eventually led to telepathy. I began to clearly receive others' thoughts and pass my thoughts to them.

Fortunately, the limping officer was not injured to the point of not being able to continue, and we dropped him back off with his grateful boat crew and continued on to the next evolution. This officer continued on through the rest of training with his class and went on to be a great leader in the teams.

There are times when the higher self will come through and nudge you in a particular direction, and you won't know it at the time until you look back over events that have transpired. At other times, you will get the nudge from your higher self before events transpire. I have learned to detect when I am being nudged by my higher self and have been fortunate to be given insights that have prevented the loss of my life and the lives of others. In this case, it resulted in bending a little to help mold a quality future leader. Thoughts are powerful things and can be picked up by others, knowingly or unknowingly. It happens at sporting events between opposing teams. I remember playing soccer and football in high school and being able to know when people were about to tackle me or try and take the ball without seeing them. In conjunction with these times, I would experience a kind of slow motion effect; the stadium stands were quiet, and I could only hear the sound of my breathing. I would move, dodge, or feint in a way that was perfect to avoid being tackled or having the ball stolen. I was picking up my opponent's thoughts just as they were about to move on me.

The effect of thoughts, either negative or positive, between countries can also have an effect. Thoughts are always being telegraphed, but, like a radio, you don't hear all the stations at once; you have to tune in to the right frequency to hear them. The same is true for thoughts. If a country's leaders and people have a positive or negative will for another country, then it will be telegraphed. In some places in the world where there is fighting, it is obvious what the intent is. This intent will remain until the leaders and people change their thoughts. It can change overnight or it can remain for millennia. We as a whole can change our thoughts to love for one another or hang on to old thought patterns of fear. We have the choice, and it is as simple as changing our thoughts.

If you intend to be connected with a person, a group, or an event, you will start to pick up on the thoughts and energy just like tuning in to a radio station as you focus your own thoughts and intentions on what you desire. Begin to notice the synchronicities that will begin to happen, and you will see the power of your thoughts unfold.

Thoughts are transmitted from your mind as demonstrated by the experiments of Cleve Backster who is the director of the premier Backster School of Lie Detection. By connecting plants with a polygraph machine, he was able to show how just the thought of harming a plant would send the lie detection machine's recording needles peaking on the graph chart. These experiments and many others are discussed in detail in the book *The Secret Life of Plants* by Peter Tompkins and Christopher Bird.

Thoughts are truly powerful, as I demonstrate in some of the courses I teach, and when filled with good intent can cause miracles to happen. Because of the power of thoughts, you should choose only the good ones, and when you catch yourself thinking negatively, change your thoughts back as quickly as possible to positive ones. Just think what the world would be like if all the world leaders understood this intuitively and used this knowledge. I believe many police officers and criminal detectives, knowingly or unknowingly, telepathically read the thoughts of criminals. I believe that as telepathy is more widely understood and used in the future, it will radically change not only our justice system, but many of the political and religious systems throughout humanity. In the meantime, telepathy or a knowing without knowing how or why certain thoughts come to us, will continue to impact more of humanity in a multitude of ways that are just beginning to unfold.

"THE MOST IMPORTANT THING IN LIFE IS TO LEARN TO GIVE
OUT LOVE, AND TO LET IT COME IN."

◊ *Morrie Schwartz* ◊

Chapter 7

TIMELESS AWARENESS

Many people throughout history have known when they were going to die and predicted their deaths through intuition. One of the most incredible stories that I have heard of in recent times is that of Morgan Stanley security chief Rick Rescorla, who intuited 9/11 six years before the attack that collapsed the Twin Towers in New York City. He made it a point to train all of the employees of Morgan Stanley in evacuation procedures that he devised in anticipation of the attack, and was there the day the towers were hit. He organized and directed the evacuation of the people he was in charge of protecting, moving up and down the stairs of the burning building, and is credited with saving 2,700 lives. Rick was a former British Para Commando who served in Vietnam and later became a U.S. citizen. He died in the collapse of the second tower and is one of the unsung heroes of that tragic event.

History is full of stories of those who had an intuitive ability bordering on precognition. The ability to see future events is one of many intuitive abilities that begin to manifest through developed intuition. I have had several precognitive events while working as a security contractor. As my ability began to improve with use, I was able to see events before they would happen, often weeks ahead of time. As my coworkers became aware of my abilities, they would half jokingly ask me to keep them informed.

I believe that future events are not written in stone and that we are predestined to live no matter what we do. Future events, like a speeding train that is moving down the tracks toward a vehicle stalled across the tracks, have a probable outcome and sometimes several possible outcomes. The vehicle stalled on the tracks looks like it would have the probable outcome of being destroyed by the onrushing train. It could have the possible outcome, which you cannot observe until it happens, of the vehicle starting at the last second and accelerating out of the way, or a vehicle from behind or in front pushing it out of the way.

Precognizant events are similar to this scenario in that the observer can have an impact on probable outcomes if he gets involved. By directing events in order to forestall or avoid a probable future outcome, a tragedy can be avoided or its impact lessened.

We are taught that time is linear and has a set, immovable, unchangeable past, present, and future. Quantum physics has demonstrated that as observers we influence the outcome of an event by our thoughts. If we accept the possibility that we are creating our world through our thoughts, we can move toward a comprehension of the possibility of changing probable future events by our thoughts and actions.

All time, as taught by many ancient indigenous American cultures, has already happened. Past, present, and future have all happened, and we are living all of it simultaneously. Einstein theorized that if you could build a spaceship or device that could move you faster than the speed of light, you could move to different points on the time continuum and experience a past or future event in real time. If we take this theory and combine it with the ancient thought that time is all happening simultaneously, then we can begin to see a scientific and spiritual possibility for precognition.

We also know that thought has no boundary, in that we can focus on a past event and recall it in great detail. We can look ahead to the future and think about what we want to experience, such as a new car, house, partner, etc., and see after time has gone by that the thing that we focused on in the past has transpired as we saw it. All of our power is in the now moment. We can influence all events throughout time through our thoughts in the now moment.

For instance, we now collectively believe that Atlantis is a myth. If, as a collective, we became aware that this is not a myth, then all the information that is currently available that points to Atlantis being a reality would quickly unfold. New information would then quickly come forward that would solidify this, and we would have thus changed our past through our now.

If a precognizant individual came forward, and I'll use my real life events as an example, and said at such a time and place, by a particular mode of delivery, an attack would occur, and he convinced those who had the ability to make adjustments to prevent this attack, then we would have changed the future through our now. It's really not rocket science, but it is a combination of science and spiritual knowledge.

I remember an occasion when I was on a predicting streak of seeing terrorist attacks a week ahead of time in the city I was working in. I had pointed out two attacks that were coming one week after the other that were both spectacular with great loss of life. Everyone took notice in my group, and we decided to try and influence the next attack that I saw happening within the next week. This next attack I saw coming was at the location where many of us lived. The person that we were in charge of protecting decided to relay to security personnel that it was revealed that an attack was coming to our residence. They were told that security was already heightened in the city because of the previous bombings, and that it was suffi-cient. We were also told that no specific threats had come in, so an increase in security was not justified.

Within an hour of that meeting, a retired general who lived close to our location phoned in to inform our security head that suspicious people had come randomly to his house and asked where the Americans were. Within a couple of hours, security was beefed up around our residence. It was now just twelve hours until my intuition and precognitive vision had determined an attack would take place. I was disappointed in the security arrangements, however, and felt that the attack would still be successful. I had given my thoughts on what would work, but they were discounted by the security chief as too excessive. As a precaution, a few of us from our group moved out and into temporary quarters. A few of the ones left behind were going to get up very early the next morning before the attack and leave. That would unfortunately leave a few people in rooms that were out of the direct threat of the blast I saw coming, but still potentially in danger of injury. Other people within the building and the security force outside would be wiped out in the blast.

That night, I slept a fitful sleep and got up several hours early, before the imminent attack that I knew was coming between seven and eight in the morning. I wanted to do something to try and stop the attack, so I began to meditate. Stilling the mind had always worked for me, even in life-or-death training situations. I had been in several while I was a Navy SEAL, and to work myself out of them, I had stilled my mind and the right solution had miraculously come through. I had learned some excellent meditation techniques, and I applied them now. I stilled the thoughts in my mind and relaxed the tension I felt in my body. I focused on one thought, which was how to counter the coming attack.

After a while, I began to see a young man who was driving toward our residence. I saw him as if I were in the car with him. I could hear his thoughts as if he were speaking them out loud. I felt compassion for this poor misguided soul who was convinced he was doing the right thing by killing innocent people. I know that free will is the God-given right of every soul on earth, and to interfere with this free will without another's consent is a crime in the spiritual realms. I could read this young man's thoughts of how he was regretting that he had not had the opportunity to experience love and marriage. My thoughts then turned to love and how by beaming the energy of love I had been able to protect groups. I now started doing the same thing to this suicide bomber. I would send him love to help bring him out of the fear and negative vibration he was trapped in. I continued thinking love and sending it out to this man as the hour at which I had seen the explosion occurring approached.

About twenty minutes before the time at which the explosion was predicted to take place, I began to feel a release as if a tension within my gut was unwinding. As the time for the explosion came and went, I knew that something had changed the probable bombing into a nonevent. I felt relief and left my room to see how the others in our group were. They had felt the same tension in the gut that I had and had simultaneously felt it release and had felt the same relief that I did. A couple of the people, I later found out, had been praying with similar results of tension and relief at the same time. Thoughts, whether prayers or love energy, are capable of miraculous results, as has been seen throughout history.

I would continue to point out likely attacks and report them. We would later find out that several of these resulted in arrests of individuals who were actually planning on carrying out these attacks. Security was beefed up in locations where I said that attacks would occur, and they ended up not happening.

This event that I have described was another important moment in my life, as I was now able to travel by thought into the future and change a possible outcome. The Western intellect has a hard time grasping the full power that would present itself if commingled with Eastern thought. I believe this story can help change that.

Intuitive people throughout time have predicted events that later turned out not to happen. I don't take every prediction I hear at face value anymore, even if it is from a highly reputable source. I now know that people can change a probable outcome into another possibility if they focus enough energy on it.

Take weather for instance. Weather prediction has radically improved over the last several decades, with technological advances in supercomputers and satellites. Even with these advances, we still cannot predict with 100 percent accuracy what a weather pattern will do. There have been hurricanes that were given a high probability of landing at certain locations but turned their track and headed out to sea, where little impact was felt. It has been revealed that group prayer turned some of these storms.

Because we don't currently accept the capability of thought to influence events, do we completely discount it when we are told that people were focused on negating these storms? When the media begins coverage of massive storms and tells millions of viewers that great destruction is going to happen when these storms touch down in a specific area, do we not discount that fear can have a possible effect? What if the media reported these events and said that the probability is great right now that these storms will land, but it is possible that it could be diverted into the open sea at this point in its development if enough people projected their thought at it? How far away from this happening are we? We can change our environment, but it will take the mingling of the Eastern and Western mindsets to make it happen. The local, or Western, mind and the non-local, or Eastern, mind combined can heavily influence outcomes. Local reality is our physical world, and non-local reality is the world of intuition. I have used my thoughts to influence the weather, like the shaman from indigenous cultures who can call in rain.

I have also had incredible success bringing in or diverting weather patterns with my thought intention. Areas that I have been to that have had severe drought have had unpredicted rain or snowfall. I have diverted storms and known when weather was coming. It all starts with a desire, a focus, and a belief.

I am not alone in this ability of changing my environment. I attended a course on dowsing recently by a unique gentleman named Raymond Grace. Raymond teaches in a down-to-earth style that is characteristic of his way of life. He teaches dowsing, which is normally taking a forked stick and using it as a device for sensing underground water sources, minerals, or magnetic earth fields. However, Raymond teaches dowsing in a form that shows you how to change the energetic flow of people, places, and situations. I saw a kindred spirit in this amazing and kindly fellow, and we began talking between lectures. Turns out, we were doing the same thing as far as changing our environments through thought energy. He is a healer on many different levels, and one of the many things he taught the class over a two-day period was how we could change the energy of polluted water by scrambling the negative energy contained in it to make it pure. He is involved in several projects, one of which, according to his foundation's web site is to make information available to help people learn to improve the quality of their drinking water, create a positive environment in their schools, and achieve goals.

Powerful spiritual teachers have taught us throughout time to focus on love, peace, forgiveness, and compassion. I believe that if we were to truly abide by these teachings, we would stop wars, crime, disease, and pollution. Thoughts are powerful; choose only the good ones.

"WERE THERE NO INNER SIGHT OR INTUITION, THE JEWS WOULD NEVER HAVE HAD THEIR BIBLE, NOR THE CHRISTIANS JESUS. WHAT BOTH MOSES AND JESUS GAVE TO THE WORLD WAS THE FRUIT OF THEIR INTUITION OR ILLUMINATION."

◊ *H.P. Blavatsky* ◊

Chapter 8

AN INTERNAL KNOWING

Most people are prompted with an internal knowing, nudge, or intuition throughout their day, without being aware of or acknowledging the possibility of its existence or just dismissing its subtle nudges. These nudges are part of the higher self centered in the heart trying to communicate with the conscious mind. If we were to recognize our internal nudges as they happen in our lives and acknowledge them in others, we would open many doors into higher states of consciousness that could greatly enhance our life experiences. Internal insights have literally saved my life and the lives of many people I have worked with countless times over the years. By my using these internal promptings, believing in them, and acting on them, I have been fortunate, despite having worked in extremely high-risk areas, to never have any serious injuries happen to me, my teams, or any of the people we were protecting. Imagine if everyone in the groups I've been involved with understood and applied their internal knowing and worked together to build upon and utilize the group's internal promptings; imagine how much more cohesive, resourceful, and effective the group could be.

I was on the Ambassador Bremer detail in Iraq in December 2003 and was left in charge of the protection detail while Ambassador Bremer and our detail head went back to the states for Christmas break. He was a busy man while in charge and kept us busy morning to night providing his security as he traveled all over Baghdad and throughout Iraq, helping to establish the new Iraqi government. While on his Christmas break, some of us had decided to go down to Babylon to view the ancient ruins. The night before we were to go down for our visit, I got the first of what was to be many "hits" from my higher self, as I would call my intuitive nudges, that we would be in danger if we went. Up until this point, Iraq was a relatively safe place, and the town of Hilla, where the ancient city of Babylon was located, was and always had been safe. I decided to call everyone and cancel the move with the excuse that logistical problems had occurred. I was in charge of everyone's safety, and if I felt something was unsafe, then it was my responsibility to make the call. The next day, the day that we were to go to Hilla, there was the first attack in that area since the ground invasion almost a year earlier. Polish soldiers were killed as a result, and if I had not called off the trip, we would have been in the middle of it. My next "hit" would come soon after that one.

A couple of days later, we were scheduled to go to a range just outside the green zone that we had used on several random occasions to site in our weapons and keep ourselves tuned up on weapons use.

We were supposed to go out the gate to the range at a certain time, which was 0800 in the morning. I had gotten another "Intuitive Hit" the night before and was trying to figure out how I could delay our move and stall for time. Fortunately, some of the guys were late showing up. Then I told everyone I wanted to give a good range brief before we went; these two things delayed us for some time. I wasn't sure why I needed to stall for time; I just knew that we didn't need to be going through the gate to the range at our prearranged time. The answer was given when at about the same time we would have been rolling through the gate, a huge explosive shock wave shook the presidential palace where we had our office. Several of us went to the roof to check out what had happened and saw a large amount of black smoke rising from the gate area we would have been traveling through at the time the explosion happened. Sirens began to wail, and there was a lot of commotion around the palace grounds. We were soon to learn that a suicide car bomb had gone off right in front of the gate we were to have been traveling through. It was the first suicide car bomb in Iraq, and no one up to that point had any indication that it was even a remote possibility. I knew because I would go to intelligence briefings every day to find out what was going on, not just in Baghdad but the whole country, and nothing had been indicated through intelligence that this attack was coming. This bombing caused the loss of almost one hundred innocent Iraqi lives that were traveling through the intersection outside the gate where the attack occurred or in the long line of cars that were waiting to come in through the gate's security checkpoint.

At first I did not share my insights with others. I just moved events, times, or travel routes around so that we would avoid the unsafe areas that I was getting "intuitive hits" about. I would struggle for a while at accepting these insights. This internal struggle was amazing, because no matter how often I would get insights that were confirmed, I still questioned them and would struggle internally with whether they were accurate, instead of accepting them and adjusting to allow these insights to help me and the people I was protecting. These insights were at first just seconds, minutes, or a day before something happened, but as I began to finally accept and allow them, they became more accurate and gave me a longer time frame before the events.

My intuition was evolving and becoming quite good at alerting me when I was getting close to a dangerous area by giving me a strong feeling that I was definitely in danger and these would normally be confirmed by an attack. Eventually, I would get feelings of danger far enough in advance and would avoid an area but not get any immediate feedback whether it was a correct intuitive signal. But, sure enough, I would eventually find out about an attack in the local papers, news broadcasts, intelligence reports, or accounts from other contractors or military units. At certain times in Iraq, the violence and attacks became so frequent and widespread that not all the attacks were reported or cataloged. I would eventually find out that an attack had occurred in the area and time frame that I had thought it would. So I began to trust these intuitive flashes and would start to concentrate on the feelings I would get when they would come. As I focused on these feelings, I would get a picture in my mind of a location and time frame. At this early point in my awareness of this ability, I did not excessively question how this was happening because by questioning and doubting I had learned that the intuitive ability will begin to diminish in its ability to give me ample warning to evade an area or time frame.

These insights did not control my life, and I would go for long periods of time sometimes without a "hit," but when they came, I paid attention to the guidance they were giving. I still used the analytical side of my brain by determining, through attack patterns and locations of attacks, when and where possible attacks might take place, but I found that along with my intuitive side, I became quite effective at avoiding and predicting future attacks.

To develop this inherent skill which all humans possess, I had first become aware of it in others, and through observation had established that it was indeed a trait that had developed in individuals for one reason or another. I learned that if others are to develop this capability, they must first accept the possibility that it exists. From that point forward, they can begin to be aware of it in themselves and thus begin tapping into the higher self and the limitless potential that entails.

My intuitive side really started to develop because of a desire to anticipate what others were doing and thinking during training missions in the SEAL teams. The SEAL teams are constantly honing and developing their skills, and we would have exercises and training missions every week. We would work on certain skill areas over a period of about a month, and then move to another. One month might be diving skills, and the next land warfare. After training for a few weeks on a particular skill, we would challenge the skill developed and honed in us by having aggressor teams look for us during a full mission profile that incorporated many different skills, including the one we had concentrated on.

Sometimes I would be the aggressor, but whatever side you were on, it always turned out to be a battle of wits as you tried to sneak around and pull off something out of the ordinary to really challenge the other group. If we were going against each other, it was always hard because we could really push the envelope on creativity. It was during some of these training evolutions that I would get my first taste of seeing others perform amazing things, and I would start doing them as well.

I remember the first time that I tried to remote view a path to see what was on the path. I closed my eyes and relaxed into a meditative state, and in my mind's eye could see the path and the dips in it, the turns in the path, branches from a tree, and water on the path. I had never been on this path in the woods before and was skeptical because there had been no rain in the area for over a week. I started down the path and saw the three dips that I had envisioned, the twist by a large tree whose branches reached across the path like I had seen in my visualization, and there was the water that I had not believed in, in the form of a small stream.

Our imaginations and reality are thought to be two distinct and separate entities, but they are actually not very different. The problem lies in our ability to comprehend them as similar. Our imaginations work outside the linear time/space continuum that we are aware of, outside our current accepted reality. Our imaginations are free of the restrictions we put upon them with our rigid adherence to linear time and space. Our imaginations roam freely through dimensions and know no linear time.

It was not as hard for me to make the transition as I would have previously thought, because everything within the SEAL teams' training pushes you far beyond the accepted norm. Creativity and leadership are encouraged at even the most junior rank, with the most junior guy running full mission profiles at times. The impossible challenge makes a SEAL grin with delight and starts the internal wheels turning, because we have learned countless times how to overcome insurmountable obstacles. I was fortunate to be in good company and learn from masters of many different abilities. It is said that when the student is ready, the master will appear, and I was a student my whole twenty-four-year career as a SEAL. No matter how advanced I became, I was always ready to learn more, and would learn on many occasions, from the most junior of the men among us. The teacher, I would find throughout my career, and today as I teach, often learns as much as the student. This is because you are constantly watching, adjusting, guiding, and motivating in new ways as you teach.

I continued to play with my newfound skill of remote viewing and learned that if I focused on my initial vision of the landscape ahead, I would get the most accurate idea of what it was. The ego always wants to be in charge, so you have to be aware of its little tricks. After receiving the initial vision of the landscape ahead, the ego would always try and play the doubting game or give me a separate vision, which it was creating. If you allow your ego to run your life, which most people unwittingly do, then it will give you an image that is false or try to use twisted logic to try and break your resolve to develop your new way of perceiving your world. Put the ego in its rightful place as developer of your personality, not as the one running the show, and then you will be able to develop your intuition. After receiving an image, I would check it for accuracy. As you learn to filter the noise out of your intuitions, you will start to fine-tune them and become confident in your ability with intuition. I found that at first I needed to meditate and quiet my mind to access the creative ability of the alpha waves. Once in this "alpha" mode, I would shift into visualizing the landscape ahead.

Like working a muscle, you train your intuition a little at a time. Overtraining will start to give you false results, because the mind will start to create random patterns to satisfy your search. In a relaxed state of mind, you will get the visuals, but forcing it will give you false readings. As I trained my imagination to become productive and bring me real information instead of created information, I started to reach out further and further with my search of the landscape. I spend a lot of time driving, as I like to explore and visit historical sites and museums around the U.S., and when I travel around the world I do a lot of driving as well, so I started remote viewing while I drove. After a while, I got really good at it and started to play a game of searching for where the speed traps were. I got really good at this as well, and although I don't speed when driving, I've learned to put this on automatic search mode as a safety precaution in case my speed drifts higher, but most importantly because many people react by hitting their breaks when they see a speed trap, which can be quite dangerous (and a nuisance when some people feel they need to adjust their speed below the speed limit, which is not what speed traps are designed for).

You can program your intuition to do anything. The finest example of "intuition in action" is mothers with young children. I remember once when I was visiting my parents with my son who was five months old at the time. My son was crawling around, happily exploring his new environment, when he started to choke. My parents and I were stopped in mid conversation, and I went over and concernedly picked up my son to see what was happening. I have been highly trained in medical emergencies as a SEAL and was going through my mind what steps I would take when out of a back room came his mother and without the slightest hesitation did a finger sweep down the boy's throat and pulled out a small piece of pine cone. My mother had an ornamental display of pinecones and he had probably found a piece on the floor and tried to eat it.

His mother had just gotten up, without hearing anything—she was in a back room where the sound from the room we were in didn't penetrate—and with very little medical training had done the most perfect thing for this situation. It happened in a flash, and my son was fine and went back to playing without missing a beat.

Other examples of intuition most people will admit to having experienced are when a close friend or family member will call or visit out of the blue. Usually you will hear the surprised "I was just thinking of you." That's how intuition works in our everyday lives. A more recent intuitive flash that I received was to pull all the funds out of my IRA accounts in early February of 2008. I have been an investor for more than thirty years, so this flew in the face of all reason, because the market was up by a big percentage and most investment advisors were saying it was going to remain high or go higher. But I've learned to trust these intuitive "hits," and this was a big one. To date, this saved me more than 70 percent of my IRA savings. I took a big hit in the last dotcom meltdown and was glad not to have gotten slammed in the one happening in the late 2000s. I would not be surprised if on hindsight I will be even happier that I pulled all of my funds from all of my accounts. This is another example of putting your intuition into auto-search mode. I had not wanted to pull my funds, and logic was against this, but when you trust your intuition and it saves your life or others' lives, why not focus it into other aspects of your life?

You can use your intuition in any and or all aspects of your life. All you need to do is ask and wait for the response. If you ask from your head, I've learned that the response can be accurate, but the best and most pure responses will come from the heart. The heart has been found to actually contain neurons similar to the brain. The Institute of HeartMath has mapped the electromagnetic fields of the brain and heart, and the heart's field is far broader than the brain's.

The science of the heart is opening up new doors, but much of this knowledge is being relearned by the West because indigenous tribes have been connected to the heart for many ages. As we come to accept our ability to intuit outside of our three-dimensional, linear-time reality, we will learn to intuit on greater and greater levels.

I know I've pushed the boundaries of many people's awareness of intuition and probably their ability to allow new information to enter their minds. But I want to push your limits one last time. This may be over the top for many, but if nothing else, consider that what

I tell you may be possible. I have found that when I intuit something negative that's coming in the future, I can change its outcome if I do it from the heart.

Everything that happens in our time/space reality has probabilities and possibilities. There have been several times over the last couple of years when I have attracted a different possibility instead of the negative one that was going to happen. At first I started getting bold and telling people that I worked with that I was getting an intuitive hit that an attack was coming. It was just with the core group of people that I worked with and trusted initially, but after I got comfortable with this, I worked it up the chain of command. Once they started getting comfortable with my accuracy, they started informing the right people to stop attacks before they even happened. They would set up security so tight that the attacks could not occur, or they would conduct a sting operation and nab the people about to commit the attacks or intercept them on their way. I eventually progressed to the point where I would send the love vibration to the attackers that I could see in my visions, and they would change their minds and find other targets or I would stop the entire group during their planning.

This was a long process that I went through to get to the point of changing a future event, and had tried to actually use force in the etheric realm very early on when I detected who was actually master-minding the attacks in Iraq, but that was trying to use darkness on darkness, so it was actually more negative. I learned that the most effective way was to use the heart and send the thought of love and light to bring light to darkness; that was the trick that turned the tide on upcoming events that I could see were about to affect me and the team of contractors I was working with.

All of humanity is intuitive and can develop and master this ability; the only thing that impedes the process is the knowledge that it is part of us. Imagine a world where everyone accepted this as reality and all of our dealings with each other were on this level. I would love to teach this to our political leaders and families so that they could operate our country from the place of intuition instead of the place of ego.

"THROUGH THE TRAVAIL OF THE AGES, MIDST THE POMP AND TOIL OF WAR, HAVE I FOUGHT AND STROVE AND PERISHED COUNTLESS TIMES UPON THIS STAR. SO AS THROUGH A GLASS, AND DARKLY THE AGE LONG STRIFE I SEE, WHERE I FOUGHT IN MANY GUISES, MANY NAMES, BUT ALWAYS ME."

◇ *General George S. Patton* ◇
(From Through a Glass, Darkly)

Chapter 9

THE MIND OF A NAVY SEAL

I had played with toy soldiers from some of my earliest recollections of around three years old. I would play with them for hours on end as they fought and toiled, won and lost battles. I believe my mother must have loved the way I would quietly entertain myself for long stretches of time. I would create elaborate battlefields outside that would take hours to construct, or, if inside, I would create them in my mind like some vaguely remembered dream. I watched TV shows like *Combat* with Vic Morrow or movies like *The Vikings* with Kirk Douglas, and was enthralled and eagerly anticipated the next time I could watch them again. I could see myself fighting battle after battle with them as if I was actually there.

I remember begging my mother for weeks for a large tank that was battery operated and large enough that I could ride on it. I never really expected to get it, but would longingly stare at it as we passed day after day on our way to and from our home. I probably left many fingerprints and nose prints on that window, looking at that tank. I remember one day we actually went into the store, and my heart leaped for joy because I was sure my mother was going to get the tank for me. The store manager must have seen me looking at the tank over the weeks because he came forward with a big smile, but was intercepted by my mother and pulled away, leaving me to stare at the tank. I marveled in its design and power. Alas, we walked out of the store without the tank, and I was crestfallen. I finally gave up on the idea of ever having the tank and was surprised as we passed the store that it was still there after many more weeks went by. My mother surprised me one day by bringing home the cherished tank, and I played on and with it for as long as allowed. It eventually quit working as most things made in Japan did at the time, but I still played with it. I would imagine I worked with General Patton and the first American tank core set up during WWI as I played with my giant tank. I could picture myself riding the tank into battle, dueling with opposing cannon, and leading the infantry to victory over the enemy.

When I was old enough to read, I would religiously read the comic book exploits of Sgt. Rock as he and his group of men would travel over the European countryside, fighting the Germans. It was after reading these comics for years that in one of these issues I read a rare extra insert on the exploits of a Navy frogman. He swam on the surface to do a reconnaissance of Japanese fighting fortifications on a Pacific island and threw a haversack of explosives at a pillbox and destroyed it after he came under fire. Later, he was swimming underwater with scuba gear and detected an enemy submarine secretly lying on the bottom, waiting for ships to go by. The frogman swam down and placed a limpet mine on the side of the hull and blew it up. I was hooked, and from that moment on I knew what I was going to do when I grew up.

One of my favorite movies as a boy was *Patton* with George C. Scott playing the lead role, for which he won an Oscar. I remember one scene in which old "Blood and Guts" was driving in a jeep to a battlefront when he told his driver to make a quick turn up ahead that was in a different direction from the front. After a short argument over directions, they made the turn and came upon some Romanesque ruins where the battle of Zama was fought. Echoing and fading trumpets add to the haunting scene as Patton recounts, "It was here. The battlefield was here. The Carthaginians defending the city were attacked by three Roman legions. Carthaginians were proud and brave, but they couldn't hold. They were massacred. Arab women stripped them of their tunics and their swords and lances. The soldiers lay naked in the sun, two thousand years ago, and I was here." Patton said that he believed he was Hannibal of Carthage reincarnated, and the similarities, both physical and tactical, are amazing.

If I had past lives, I could see myself at the battle of Thermopylae as a Spartan, or with Alexander the Great as he conquered the known world. The SEAL teams' training and martial philosophy is similar to the Greeks in that physical conditioning, discipline, and tactical capabilities are very finely and consistently honed.

Many of the military geniuses of the past intuitively knew when and where to direct resources and men at the crucial time to win battles and turn the tide of war to achieve victory. I was fortunate to wind up in an organization that has a history of intuitive decision-making that has made the SEAL teams famous today. From the intuitive decision by President Kennedy in 1961 to start the SEAL teams to the most recent decision by President Obama to use SEALs to rescue a captured American Maritime Captain from pirates, the SEAL teams have proven to be decisive and dependable intuitive warriors.

I believe that the extensive traveling to the Far and Middle East that I have experienced as a SEAL and security contractor has had an influence on the way that I process information, and has helped develop my intuitive abilities. The way information and experiences are processed in the East is different from the Western world. They experience life from a more spiritual aspect, whereas the West is more analytical. Neither is better than the other, but when both are utilized, you walk between worlds, so to speak. This allows you to experience a fuller aspect of our world.

I have worked on both coasts of the United States where the SEAL teams are located. I believe that because of the experiences that SEALs on each coast are exposed to, they are shaped internally differently. While there is some kidding about the professional capabilities between the different coasts, I have found that on both coasts the SEAL teams are exceptional warriors. While each coast specializes in certain geographical areas, what is it that makes them all special?

Many authors have probed this question, but most have been outside the organization they searched for answers from. The authors that were former SEALs have written about their experiences, and have given many exciting tales of adventure, but have not given us insight into what really makes a SEAL unique.

My experiences and reflections, both as a SEAL for over twenty-four years and now as a security contractor for more than six years, looking back in from the outside, have given me insights that I did not have while in the teams. I believe that the way SEALs, especially the advanced and more mature operators, process information is the key to their amazing capabilities. The mind must be prepared to receive information, and the intense training that we continually go through in the teams helps stimulate the creative process. In our training missions, we are constantly exposed to dangerous situations. Whether jumping out of airplanes at thirty thousand feet with oxygen and gear strapped on and freefalling down to two thousand five hundred feet before you pull your freefall parachute, swimming in shark infested waters off the coast of Somalia, shooting different weapons at night in close proximity to others in rugged terrain while moving, or driving our boats in storm-tossed seas to rocky shorelines, a SEAL must be ready to creatively handle the problems that always crop up.

I have been in just as many life and death situations in simulated combat training as I have in real combat. There is nothing like the prospect of death staring you in the face to get your attention and help you make a decision to react or die. This constant hazardous training pushes you into the creative right brain to the point where it is second nature. This is one of the major attributes of a SEAL and, in my opinion, what the success of any operation, whether simulated or real world combat, depends on. The creative ability combined with intense discipline creates a superwarrior. A warrior that can do what others would call superhuman feats. When combined with like-minded warriors, you can accomplish what others dare not or wouldn't even conceive of.

An individual must be open-minded for thoughts and ideas to take hold. As a SEAL, you must be open to the thoughts and ideas of the most junior man, because he could possibly be the subject matter expert, depending on what you are doing. The SEAL teams are not a rigidly hierarchical organization, and because of this, the creative aspect is encouraged to evolve.

My martial arts training also opened my mind further, as the advanced aspects of this information not only access the analytical side, but also the creative side. I was involved in Sayoc Kali blade fighting toward the latter part of my career as a SEAL. This martial training took me to a far higher level of awareness as a warrior. It's not unusual to have moments of deep enlightenment when pushed by intense physical training. I was fortunate to experience one of these moments one night during a secret advanced Sayoc Kali test, which is held for only a select few.

Other aspects that evolve the creative aspects of the mind of a SEAL are the travel to distant, exotic lands. Often the places that SEALs go to are remote, and because of this they are able to interact with simple and sometimes primitive peoples. Many of these people are still connected with the earth and the rhythms of life are much slower. Being exposed to this way of thinking and environment can have a positive effect on your thinking patterns.

Brain wave rhythms that are creative vibrate at the rate of running water as in streams, rivers, and the ocean. SEALs are constantly on, next to, or near water most of the time, because our specialty is to work in this environment. Many people have water fountains in their homes for this reason and because it is relaxing. Spending time at the beach, river, or lake is common for many people, and the natural rhythms are a major reason. Looking into a fish tank will also stimulate these rhythms, as will looking into a flame or a fire. That's why you can see people go into a trace-like state when watching a fire. Their brain waves are matching the vibrations of the flames. They are stimulating the creative side, or their right brain.

Being exposed to remote areas that are still very natural can also have a positive effect on brain wave patterns, in that they are also vibrating at the creative cyclic rate. Schumann waves, which are global electromagnetic resonances, are earth's base frequency, or heartbeat, and are measured at 7.8 cycles per second Hz. Alpha brain waves as measured by an electroencephalogram range between 7-12 Hz. The lower the range, the deeper into a relaxed meditative state you go. As you are exposed to longer periods in these environments, and you remain quiet, your brain will start to entrain, or match the vibration of the earth's Schumann resonance.

So, there are several different things that develop a SEAL into one of the premier Special Forces units on the planet.

1. Middle and Far Eastern philosophies that focus on creative right brain thinking, as does the SEAL teams. This exposure can come through actual contact with these areas or through intensive martial arts training.
2. Intensive combat training and combat action.
3. Interaction with earth-connected indigenous cultures.
4. Exposure to environments that stimulate the creative side of the brain naturally, such as remote areas of ocean, jungle, mountainous terrain, forest, or desert.

If you wanted to think like a Navy SEAL, you would not necessarily have to go through the training. By exposing yourself to three or four of the above outlined points, you could experience this type of mindset, which would go a long way toward preparing you to be intuitional. Of course, you would not become an honorary SEAL even if you should find yourself thinking like a SEAL, so please don't start telling people you are. You still must go through the training and spend some time at a SEAL team before you can do that. We haven't found the right correspondence course that would suffice for distance training yet; however, this book may be close.

"THE WAY OF THE WARRIOR DOES NOT INCLUDE OTHER WAYS... BUT IF YOU KNOW THE WAY BROADLY, YOU WILL SEE IT IN EVERYTHING."

◊ *Miyamoto Musashi* ◊

Chapter 10

MARTIAL ARTS AS A MEANS FOR AWAKENING THE WARRIOR WITHIN

Growing up, I was always fascinated by martial arts and always wanted to learn some form of fighting system. I had friends who practiced many different styles, and they would show me moves. I enjoyed learning them, but I never actually got to formally study a system until I entered the UDT/SEAL Teams. I started training and sparring with several teammates while deployed overseas, and I slowly started advancing my knowledge and skills. However, I still could not find anything that fully satisfied me and only peripherally learned a few advanced skills and moves.

I did not get more formalized training until I went to SEAL Team Six and began working with a contracted instructor who taught Jeet Kune Do (JKD), the system that Bruce Lee had developed. I began to really take to this system and felt that it was what I was looking for. I am very physical and liked the aggressiveness of the style; in fact, it had been developed to incorporate several different styles with the most aggressive parts of those styles rolled into one system. The movements were simple to learn, very direct and to the point and easy to excel at. Several of my teammates and I became devoted students, and a couple of guys even went on to found their own schools later.

I left SEAL Team Six and went on to our training command; after a couple years there, I volunteered to begin training in an aggressive combat fighting system for a month. For ten hours a day, every day, for thirty straight days, another SEAL from the training command and I trained in this fighting system. We were told that the hours and intensity of our training were the equivalent of a black belt of a high degree by any system's standards. We trained to fight in any terrain, with or without gear, and with or without many different weapons. We even learned to fight on and under the water. The system was very effective, and we learned many incredible ways to manipulate the human body. We could control someone with two fingers or take a life with our bare hands, and everything in between. We learned to fight multiple attackers, remove a sentry silently, handle and control prisoners, and much more. The intent was for us to eventually train the BUD/S students, which is what we did. We went through some growing pains in the beginning, as our commander at the time was opposed to martial arts of any kind and therefore put a stop to our training.

Fortunately, he was open minded, and after a group of senior personnel and myself sat down with him and convinced him to a least take a look at the training I was conducting, and then make a judgment on whether to go forward with the training, he agreed to it. I always began the initial hand-to-hand training with a classroom session that covered how to be an aggressive fighter, by using positive words and thought patterns that were very straightforward and fit in with our training as SEALs. After reviewing my classroom session and watching the aggressive moves that I was teaching the students, I was given the green light to go ahead.

After teaching the BUD/S students for several months, I started getting calls from my fellow teammates in the SEAL Teams to put something together for training them as well. I convinced the training command to fund four more guys to go through the initial one-month course I went through and then to send four of us to an advanced course that was also one month long and to be held at our remote training site on San Clemente Island off the California coast. This would allow us to fully submerse ourselves in the training and reach an even higher level of expertise. The training we received was some of the most intense training I have ever experienced. We trained for ten to twelve hours every day for thirty straight days. We were creating habits by training this long, which are like brushing our teeth or driving home from work on the same route every day, to the point where we don't need to put a conscious effort into it anymore. Our fighting was becoming reflexive to the point where no matter how we were attacked or by how many people, daytime, nighttime, in the water, on land, with or without gear, with different weapons, or a different speed of attack, we were able to instantly turn an attack and defeat our attackers. We also learned different techniques for teaching and how to transform a novice group of fighters into a highly effective fighting group after just one week, and eventually we would put together a one-month course that was geared to the Special Forces warrior.

I was fortunate over the next several years to study under some of the most renowned martial artists of the time and learn several highly aggressive systems. We were constantly evolving our system and putting the most aggressive fighting information we could find into our courses.

We would become our admiral's favorite tool for demonstrations to show off SEAL team capabilities. I would be the spokesperson for our group of instructors, and usually around the time we had a class trained to a high level, we would be giving demonstrations to high-level officers from all services, and even to congressmen. But the highlight was when we were flown all the way from the west coast to the east coast for a special demonstration for the secretary of defense. We had a great admiral and force master chief who completely supported us during our development, and it was one of those synchronistic times when everything just opened up for us. Our fighting courses were the fastest courses in the history of Commander Naval Education and Training's (CNET) command to be approved. It took us just eight months from writing the course curriculum to approval. Curriculum development alone can take an average group six months to a year to complete, and it usually takes three to five years to get a new course approved. We had a lot of good people behind this idea, and unfortunately we had a few detractors. Some comments we would hear would be "Why do I need to learn hand-to-hand when I have a gun?" To me this was a Neanderthal attitude whose time was over. You should always use the least amount of force necessary to handle a dispute. If, as a warrior, all I know to do during a dispute is to shoot, then is it any wonder why we have horrible civilian death tolls in wars?

Another issue and argument we used to implement the new courses was prisoner handling. I remember during the Panama invasion when I was the only one on a ship during a ship boarding operation. We were using the special boat unit's boats, and the lead boat that I was on came in too fast and the bumper that was on the boat caused the boat to bounce off as I leaped onto the ship. The boat had to make another pass, which took about twenty seconds, which is a lifetime in an operation like this. The ship we were boarding was in the bay just before the first lock of the canal on the Atlantic side, and was suspected of holding smuggled weapons. I moved to my position outside the bridge house of the boat to set up and wait for the rest of the boarding party. I saw a dark shape begin to approach the open door from inside the ship and pointed my gun toward the shape as it came toward me. Many thoughts ran through my mind in a blur, and one of them was, *I really haven't had any training for this type of situation.* Fortunately, the man who came out with his hands raised was a small indigenous Indian who was completely compliant and got down on the ground when I motioned. He was quickly searched and flex cuffed, then the rest of the group showed up and we went on to clear the ship. I would have a burning desire to learn better prisoner handling skills and to become proficient in hand-to-hand operations.

I was always told that everyone thought that Special Forces guys were all expert at hand-to- hand, but this was not the case until we set up the first course in the mid 1990s. Even to this day, it is still not integrated into training to the degree that it should be.

So how does martial arts training, with its inherent violence, contribute to a higher state of awareness and an awakening of our higher selves? For me, it began as I started to notice an inner calm when I began to reach the more advanced stages of fighting. This inner calm was necessary to process the information that was coming at me in rapid succession so that I could access higher states of consciousness. This inner calm only comes through a relaxed state of mind, which goes against the grain of how we are programmed through society. This inner calm that I learned through martial arts started to translate to every other aspect of my life so that many of the things that used to upset my emotional balance would no longer do so. I learned to stay balanced and focused to the point where nothing would upset me, and if it did, then I would realize it was something that I needed to work on, and I would always seem to attract these challenges over and over until I worked through them. Then they would no longer be there for me to work on and would miraculously fade out of my life, whereas before they were always popping up.

I began to see the amazing geometry in the body that eventually began to open a higher dimensional understanding of self and the universe. I saw that within and around the body is a repeating Fibonacci sequence and golden mean. I began seeing mathematical sequences unfolding when I was learning the ways in which to manipulate, control, and destroy the body in prisoner handling, grappling, and several other martial art forms through the inner workings of the skeletal system. The Fibonacci sequence and golden mean is a repeating pattern throughout life that shows up in such diverse patterns of life as seashells, flowers, fruit, art forms, such as the work of Leonardo da Vinci, and architecture like the Parthenon in Greece. Admittedly, my aspirations for learning this knowledge were not for an altruistic purpose, but over time, being exposed to greater truths began to penetrate into my awareness. It's as if humanity had denigrated to the point of violence, and higher truths had been hidden deep within violence to eventually awaken in a few that were willing to discipline themselves through sacrifice and hard work. I had found those higher truths as I went deeper into the martial arts world. Many of the greatest martial arts teachers and warriors are very balanced and calm. Of course, these calm and philosophical teachers who would seem vulnerable to the uninitiated can pull out some serious hurt if they are pushed to the limit, but it would be a rare event that you would find them in a combat situation.

There are many stories throughout time that cover martial artists who have reached a higher level of awareness through perfecting themselves with the intention of becoming better warriors. Many have become great statesmen, philosophers, artists, and teachers of the likes of Alexander the Great, Sun Tzu, Miyamoto Musashi, and many more too numerous to mention but all worthy of admiration and respect.

The deeper I went into the hard styles of martial arts, the more I awakened the inner warrior within me. The hard styles are the ones wherein you learn mind-body connection through repetitious training of physical skills. The outer warrior is refined to the point where it cannot progress any further unless it finds something outside of the normal training routines of physical repetition. As a warrior searches for these skills that will refine himself or herself further, he or she will eventually find the soft styles, or internal warrior skills.

This is not to say that the internal warrior skills cannot be sought out first over the hard styles; they can, and as the energy of the earth changes, it will be the training that everyone will shift to.

The information contained within the soft styles are already to be found in many of the great martial arts, whether the instructors or students are aware of them or not. The styles that are training the internal warrior the fastest and most efficiently in my experience are

Tai Chi and Qigong. These arts are focused on the internal energy and the creation of energy within the body.

When I speak of the internal warrior, I am no longer talking of combative styles. While these arts do teach energy movements that can be used for fighting, that is not their true intent. The intent is to connect you with your own internal energy and teach you how to create more energy within yourself and how to move that energy around. To awaken the warrior within is the true calling of both individuals and humanity as a whole. Once your internal warrior is awakened, your entire being will begin to expand in ways you never imagined.

From my own personal experience, I have been able to expand from my inner nudges or intuitions to an awakening to telepathy, clairvoyance, clairaudience, and clairsentience. These abilities are an outgrowth of expanding intuitional awareness. We all are capable of these abilities, and as humanity awakens as a whole, these abilities will become more common. In fact, many people are aware of these abilities and are already using them. But just like new technology that leaps ahead of what many people are able to comprehend, people will not understand these abilities until they are shown how to use them.

These abilities are not always on, like several radio stations playing at once. They are part of me, but will not play unless I focus my intent on them or tune into them like you would a radio station. You do not have the information from a book until you focus your eyes on the page and start reading or someone reads the words to you. It's the same way for intuitive information. I don't hear people's thoughts all the time unless I'm attuned to them. I will begin to catch team members' thoughts through telepathy over a period of time because I want to create a better team-like coherence. Some people are open to this, and some are not.

When some people begin to notice that you are in sync with them, they mix it up because they are not comfortable being part of a team. They are individualistic to the point that they will sacrifice the greater good to stay individualistic. We are currently seeing the effects of this type of attitude in the economic environment, where

CEOs of large corporations are sacrificing whole companies so they themselves can remain independent and wealthy. This independent way of thinking that sacrifices the whole for the good of the individual or the few is rapidly being replaced. Martial arts helped to awaken the inner warrior in me after I searched for a better way to be an external warrior. We cannot continue to focus on the external to the exclusion of our greater internal self. By awakening the inner warrior within each of us, we actually insure our own survival in the world and our continued evolution. To ignore the inner warrior is to not advance, and the world will no longer wait for those who are either stuck or who continue to hold onto beliefs that no longer serve all humanity.

MARTIAL ARTS AS A MEANS FOR AWAKENING THE WARRIOR WITHIN

"A MIND AT PEACE, A MIND CENTERED AND NOT FOCUSED ON HARMING OTHERS, IS STRONGER THAN ANY PHYSICAL FORCE IN THE UNIVERSE."

◊ *Wayne Dyer* ◊

Chapter 11

A WARRIOR'S MINDSET

As a child, I loved the water. From my earliest memories, I remember playing in the tub for long periods of time. My favorite bath was a bubble bath, and I would play in the water until all the bubbles were gone, the water was cold, and my skin was all wrinkled up on my fingers and toes. I would have friends stay over, and we would play in the water and splash each other until my mother would come in and tell us to calm down and quit splashing water out of the tub. I remember I had a friend at the time who was a girl and the daughter of my mom's best friend from work. I was five years old and she was six, and we did everything together, including take baths and sleep in the same bed. I'm scandalized to think back and remember that we loved to play "London Bridge is falling down" in the tub. We played this game by taking turns holding our bodies above the water by putting our legs and hands up on the sides of the tub, while the other went back forth beneath, trying not to get caught when the song ended and the bridge/body came tumbling down.

I was swimming when I was six years old, and I loved to go to the beach with my family in the summer and swim in the sun-kissed ocean. I would count down the months during the school year, because I knew that the pools, lakes, streams, and, my favorite of all, the beaches off the coast of Charlestown, South Carolina, would be open and the water warm enough so that I could swim.

I always loved the way the water would float my body, and I would just lie in the water, whether it was my bathtub or the ocean, and just go to another place. I didn't know it as a meditation at the time, but it most certainly was. When given the opportunity to swim, I would continue until I was told it was time to stop.

When I was in high school, I became a lifeguard at several pools for a couple of years so that I could be close to the water. I had dreamed of becoming a Navy frogman someday because of course they were in the water all the time and I could live my dream instead of work. I joined the Navy as soon as I was eligible and began my Navy career as a hardhat diver for two reasons. Number one was so that when I was finished with the Navy I would have a trade as a commercial diver pretty easily lined up with my Navy diver experience. Second, so that UDT/SEAL training, considered some of the hardest training in the world, would be easier. I completed hardhat diver training and, after a couple of years in that line of work, went on to complete SEAL training.

Once in the SEAL teams, I got my dream fulfilled by spending time on beaches all over the world. Diving is an incredible experience, and I would eventually teach others to dive as a PADI (Professional Association of Diving Instructors) scuba diving instructor when I was stationed on the Micronesian island of Guam for a couple of years. This was by far my favorite time in the water as a diver. I would take divers down to sunken WWI and WWII wrecks that were close enough to each other that we could reach out and touch both at the same time. Everywhere we turned were tropical fish in a riot of colors that would follow us and wait for food handouts. One of my favorite spots was called the blue hole, and the water was so clear it was like floating in air. I'd sink slowly down into the large hole at sixty feet to a depth of one hundred and twenty feet, where it came out the side of a cliff, and look back up to the surface and see swimmers circling the dive boat. The water was as warm as bath water, so I didn't need a wetsuit even at one hundred and twenty feet. Just a little way from the top of the blue hole was a huge moray eel, ten feet long and purple with light blue polka dots. He lived in a hole with a million little fish that were light blue and yellow. These little fish were constantly moving in and out of his hole like they were water from a fire hose. The eel was so gentle that you could feed him by hand. You could hold out a hot dog and he would leave his hole with half his body in and half out and gently take the hot dog from your hand.

I have never thought of anything that I did when I was in the water or around it as work. I loved what I did in the military, and although it was often hard and dangerous, it was always fulfilling. Being a warrior is not always the tough, stressful job that many people have an image of. Of course it can be, if that is what you want to make it out to be, but I have mostly happy memories from my time as a warrior.

I remember once my son's second-grade class had a day when they invited parents to come share what they did for work. I came in my nice military uniform that I wore for special functions at the Naval Academy in Annapolis, where I was stationed at the time. As it turned out, the teachers wanted me to talk to all the fifth-grade classes as well as my son's second-grade class. I gave a brief intro-duction and explained what I had done in the SEAL teams, and then I opened it up for questions. I was pleasantly pleased at the caliber of these amazing holders of our future. They were all respectful and articulate, and they offered thought-provoking questions. They asked about what it was like to jump out of a plane, shoot a gun, travel all over the world, and be in a war, and they wanted to know if I had ever killed anyone. I told them that killing someone was not the aim of a true professional warrior, and that a warrior's goal is to ideally take away an enemy's ability to fight by sneaking in and disabling his capabilities. You always do your best to use the least amount of force necessary, and only when your life or the lives of the rest of your team is in danger would you take someone's life. I gave them the scenario that if they were traveling overseas and terrorists or pirates kidnapped them and held them for ransom, guys like me, who had thorough training, would come and rescue them. If possible, we would negotiate with the terrorists, but if we had to go in to save them, we would do it quickly and professionally and with the least amount of force, though sometimes, unfortunately, it becomes necessary to kill someone that meant to kill you. I then told them that fortunately I had never had to kill anyone.

I can still say that, to this day, neither I nor anyone that I have directly worked with, both as a SEAL and as a security contractor, has killed anyone. Call it luck, call it skill, call it what you will, but I have not directly or indirectly killed anyone. It's not because I have shied away from action, because I have done my best to put myself in the mix often. Sometimes this amazes me, but I quite frankly would like for this streak to continue. I have actually had people express disappointment that I don't have a body count. Others have told me that they have even heard others talk about me being a killer. This misconception could possibly stem from having been in distant gun battles several times, and like I said, I'm surprised that it didn't happen, but it's an okay thing it didn't, in my book. The Hollywood scenario of the action hero killing multiple people and walking away unscathed is a poor example that could use an updating to taking out the bad guys without anyone getting killed.

While I have fired rounds at knuckleheads with the intent to cause harm, and have ordered others to shoot at people who were shooting at us, it has never happened that I or anyone else near me has been killed. It's like the angels have been looking after both the bad guys and the groups I work with. I kind of like it that way, to be quite honest. Perhaps my intent to only kill someone if I absolutely have to has paid off and projected out. Perhaps because

I am very highly trained, this has projected out, but I somewhat doubt this one because I always seem to get humbled when I think I'm finally the toughest guy around. What I really think is happening is that I project a positive field around myself and keep my thoughts positive.

A true warrior's mindset is one of love. You love yourself and others and believe in your cause as rightful and just. I have heard of men who didn't believe in the cause they were fighting for but fought to stand by their countrymen. Though there are many reasons men have fought in the past or now, often it ends up being that a soldier really fights for the person beside him, not for the cause. War is one of the most atrocious things that men have done to each other, and this madness must stop. Killing other human beings is completely contrary to the laws of nature.

I see the mindset of a warrior and soldier as being different. A soldier is often trained to the minimum standard necessary to function on the battlefield. A warrior has been pushed through many years of training and discipline, often to far more rigorous levels than is expected of most soldiers. This rigorous training can make a distinct difference in the attitude and professionalism between the two. In the academic world, it could be compared to the difference between a vocational college and an Ivy League school like Harvard, Yale, or Princeton. I'm not saying that the warrior has the broad base of knowledge that one learns through these institutions. But as far as the study of a particular art and science and the discipline that it takes to gain knowledge of them, the warrior is an equal, or in the long run could even surpass the Ivy League education.

As a warrior, I was often challenged to think creatively to overcome insurmountable obstacles, whether physical, mental, emotional, or spiritual. I was always able to overcome them with creative intuitive thought. This ability to think outside the box is not taught in schools but must be learned in our everyday world. Usually it is learned by accident, but unfortunately it's often never learned at all or is haphazardly acquired but never fully understood.

The amount of job-related courses, schools, and personnel development that I have gone through while studying my art is equivalent to an advanced degree. I have developed curricula and taught my fellow warriors and foreign counterparts all over the world. I have read countless books and studied with many masters in my chosen art. I would not trade any of this fine education for a degree from any prestigious school in the world. For me, the satisfaction comes from the knowledge of having excelled and gained the respect of my peers. I have become a warrior through great trial and tribulation, and now I am ready to make the journey from warrior to statesman. As a statesman, I look forward to sharing my knowledge and wisdom with others. As I progress into the stage of statesman, I feel the pull of the spiritualist, which is already impacting me and will influence me as I transition through the statesman phase of my life. A statesman, whether in public office or private industry, turns his attention to serving humanity. This is where I am now drawn, because I see the development of the art of intuition as something humanity is ready for.

What is an education but the training to prepare you to do a particular job? When you complete your education, you should be ready at some level to take up arms, so to speak, and perform that duty to a high degree. I have often spoken with people of varying levels of education, and they have often told me that a college degree was simply a piece of paper. This piece of paper allowed them to enter a field in which they had absolutely no previous hands-on training. It would have been easier and far more cost effective if they had been allowed to skip the degree and just jump right in to the career.

The students of the technical fields of science, which you would think would require extensive college training have also told me that they usually start work at such a basic level that they could easily have forgone the extensive and costly training.

Much of the training in the past was done through apprenticeships in which you would find a master and study under him to learn a particular skill or vocation. This is still done today in many fields, but the accepted thought is that you must first learn the discipline to think in an organized and constructive way. Often this type of education focuses the brain to think in linear, analytical ways through structured memorization. This educational method is often ingrained over and over again until the intuitive, creative side of the brain is atrophied. I have had several friends throughout the years who have left the SEAL teams and gone on to receive degrees in various fields. What most of them tell me is that many of their schoolmates couldn't think outside of the box if their lives depended on it. They thoroughly enjoyed their time in college, although they said that much of it could have been eliminated. They all felt that the discipline and ability for creative thinking they learned in the SEAL teams put them on a level far above their classmates. They recounted to me how they would often help their classmates begin to think outside of the paradigms they were trapped in. They were often admired and sought out for their wisdom, which is related to intuition. My friends felt their wisdom was helping their classmates succeed in ways they hadn't been able to before. You don't have to become a SEAL to acquire this way of thinking. You need to begin using the creative and intuitive side of your brain. I believe that the Greeks, during the time of Socrates, Plato, and Aristotle, taught the art of intuitive and analytical thinking combined. Intuitive thought was rapidly being suppressed toward the end of Socrates' lifetime, because it was spawning too many creative minds, which were a threat to the establishment. Alexander the Great was a student of Socrates, and both were poisoned to snuff out their threat to the old ways of control and manipulation. Alexander was poisoned secretly in the city of Babylon just before he was to start out on a new expedition into the Middle East. Socrates was ordered to drink hemlock poison by the city of Athens, which he had helped to grow in regional influence by training the creative thinkers that had gone forth from his academy. The flame of this intuitive way of thinking was eventually snuffed out over time when the last Oracle of Delphi was eventually driven away.

I believe that the creative, intuitive side of the brain should be reestablished in our schools from the very beginning of the education of our children throughout the higher learning centers. Teachers should be allowed to be more creative in their curricula and teach students to be creative in how they find information. The divine feminine side of our brains has been suppressed for far too long. It is time to reawaken it and begin the flowering of our youth. The master Yeshua once said that unless you be converted and become as little children, you will not enter into the kingdom of heaven. I believe the kingdom of heaven is here on earth and can be experienced by all of humanity once the intuitive side of the brain is awakened.

"THE DAY WILL COME WHEN, AFTER HARNESSING SPACE, THE
WINDS, THE TIDES AND GRAVITATION, WE SHALL HARNESS
FOR GOD THE ENERGIES OF LOVE. AND ON THAT DAY,
FOR A SECOND TIME IN THE HISTORY OF THE WORLD, WE
SHALL HAVE DISCOVERED FIRE."

◊ *Pierre Teilhard de Chardin* ◊
"The Evolution of Chastity"

Chapter 12

LOVE AND ITS OPPOSITE, FEAR

In order to advance to our full expression as human beings, we must learn to eliminate fear from our lives and break the paradigm of limiting belief systems. Love is the most powerful force in the universe, and we can only be part of this energy if we stay focused on it and allow it into our lives. Love is the vibration energy of all creativity, and seeking knowledge—true knowledge—is a key element of growth.

Truth and the search for it have always been the quest of humanity since the awakening of intellect, which is an amazing gift. One of the failings of intellect, however, is the difficulty in discerning what the truth is and what the ego determines or desires to be true. For if the ego has dominion over the interests of an individual, or group for that matter, then truth will always be suppressed if it does not serve the interests of the ego.

A fully aware individual who follows the interests of a heart- or love-centered intellect would never allow ego to control the intellect.

Love will always be attracted to truth, and the ego will use fear to do its bidding, which is to be the dominant controller of the mind. We are not our egos, and they should never become the master, but if we allow them to assume control, we will never advance to our full potential as spiritual beings having a human experience, but instead will have a human experience with only brief glimpses of our spiritual beings.

Although the ego is important to the formation of our character in the early formative years of our development, many people never advance beyond ego. The ego controls and is controlled through fear. To break away from fear, we must become aware of the ego's need to embrace and use fear for control of the intellect and suppression of the heart, where truth and love are recognized.

Everything in creation is vibrational energy. Love is an energy that attracts; when you receive love, you want more, and you move to an energy vibration where you can attract more of it.

Fear is a vibration that repels; when you see or feel fear, you want to get away from it as fast as possible. You do not want to attract more of that which revolts you or inhibits your development as a spiritual, seeking being of the light. Fear is none of these things, and to live in fear is to not have the beauty of the light that is available for our use.

Fear is darkness, horror, dread, panic, anxiety, anger, hate, and the opposite of all that is positive and good in the world. To focus on fear or one of its forms is to invite them into your existence, and until the moment comes when you direct your intention toward that which is love, you will continue to live in fear.

Love is light, beauty, truth, order, purpose, and all that is the opposite of fear and its many manifestations. To attract love, you must think, feel, and do love. Every spiritual master that has come forward to teach us greater truths has taught that love is the greatest key to self-mastery. Love of self, love of others, and love of all things you come in contact with.

When most people think of love, they think of the emotional

aspect or the feelings that you get when focused on something or someone outside of yourself. But to project love, you must first feel love within yourself. We are told in nearly every religion that we are all God's children. So for us to focus on loving ourselves, we are experiencing that part of ourselves that is like divinity.

Love is an energy that transcends everything in existence in our world. To feel or project love is to be a part of this God energy called love, which, when felt or projected, is doing or being a part of God's will.

Buddha said, "You can search throughout the entire universe for someone who is more deserving of your love and affection than you are yourself, and that person is not to be found anywhere. You yourself, as much as anybody in the entire universe, deserve your love and affection."

Yeshua ben Joseph said, "Love the Lord your God with all your passion and prayer and intelligence. Love others as well as you love yourself."

The Prophet Muhammad said, "Allah is compassionate and loves compassion in all things."

I do not believe that God ever wanted man to have fear. Why would an omnipotent and omniscient Being possibly want to instill fear? Fear is a manmade idea used for manipulation, control, and power. These are not the qualities of a loving energy that pervades the entire universe.

When I had my first encounter with being fully cognizant of using the energy of love, which I spoke of in the first chapter, I was awestruck at the profound implications of this amazing gift. This gift of love is contained within even the smallest particle of an atom and is inherent within each of us. I instantly realized in that moment of fear of death that to turn that energy vibration instantly into love and project it outward was the way to stop the violence.

Imagine the implications if we all focused on love and projected it out as a group. I have learned to link with this positive energy and change probable outcomes of negativity into positive outcomes.

We have all heard of the power of groups getting together with a common focus and doing amazing things. I have seen this throughout my life as a warrior when, as a collective, we would pursue an objective that would seem at times to be impossible, but through focused will, determination, and teamwork we were able to prevail. The same can happen with the energy of love being directed at a common humanitarian goal.

I have read of countless groups that have come together and meditated on lowering the crime rate of a city and having results in lowering it. There have been countless stories throughout time of individuals or groups praying for a particular outcome and having miraculous results. The power of thought directed with the intent of love is amazingly powerful.

I believe that if more people realized that they are part of the infinite source of all creation and that they have direct access to this power at any moment in time, we could inspire change as a collective much more rapidly. In most cultures, we are taught throughout virtually all areas of society, be it religion, education, judiciary, politics, family, etc., that we need to focus on allowing outside forces to take care of us. We are repeatedly told that we must give all our power to an outside force if we are to be successful and be taken care of. While I believe that all the above systems are necessary and beneficial, surrendering *all* of our power to them *unquestioningly* can lead to an eventual misuse of the power we have given them.

What is our power? Our power is in our word, in our connection to the Creator, in our desire, in our ability to think and imagine. We can use any of these individually to create, or we use them all at the same time. To lose one of them is a tragedy; to lose them all is to surrender spiritual growth and become a slave.

I remember a point in the account of *The Trial and Death of Socrates* by Plato when Socrates was defending himself and he said that in his belief, the crime that they were accusing him of was having made the people of Athens *think* for themselves. Socrates could have acquiesced to the demands of the people in power and lived a quiet life, but he could not stand by and see the people of Athens that he loved turned into mindless slaves, and so he was later sentenced to death and ordered to drink hemlock. We look back on Socrates and see him as one of the greatest thinkers of all time. Why is it that so many great people end up being killed, tortured, imprisoned, maligned, or marginalized? It is because we have given up our power and then allowed others to control us through fear to the point that we become imprisoned in someone else's ideas of what is great. We have the power to think, speak our word and question, imagine something better, desire something greater, and, through our connection with the divine, we can attract and manifest it into our lives. As a group with the same ideals, we can manifest a new world. We can collectively create a world of peace, joy, and love for all, but *we* must use our power because we have free will, and if we just sit by and watch, then someone else will use it to create the world they want to create, and it may not be the one we want.

I had my first encounter with projecting love over six years ago, and now I have progressed from projecting love out to protect myself, to projecting it out to protect others. It can be done with love and a desire to help others. If most of the people want peace, joy, and love, then I can work with that and magnify it and create a bubble of energy that vibrates that desired intention. It only takes a little imagination to begin to create a better world, and anyone can have an influence.

"IF YOU WANT TO REACH A STATE OF BLISS, THEN GO BEYOND YOUR EGO AND THE INTERNAL DIALOGUE. MAKE A DECISION TO RELINQUISH THE NEED TO CONTROL, THE NEED TO BE APPROVED, AND THE NEED TO JUDGE. THOSE ARE THE THREE THINGS THE EGO IS DOING ALL THE TIME. IT'S VERY IMPORTANT TO BE AWARE OF THEM EVERY TIME THEY COME UP."

◊ *Deepak Chopra* ◊

Chapter 13

THE LITTLE DEATH

The first time I did a Native American-inspired vision quest, I had no idea of the depths that I would go into my own inner world. A vision quest is usually first performed when a boy or girl is ready to transition into adulthood, in many indigenous tribes, this occurs around the age of fourteen to fifteen years old. After that, it is performed to inspire a vision as to a question one may have about a certain aspect of one's life that seems to be an insurmountable obstacle.

At the time of my first vision quest, I was in the process of transitioning out of the military, and I desired to know if this was the correct move for me. I loved my time in the military and had many amazing adventures, but I was feeling the time was right to move on to something new. I had chosen to do the vision quest in a group experience with an organization called Earth- Heart that basically did all the groundwork for you by setting up a safe and secure site and providing instruction and insight, as well as protection while in your vision quest area and fresh water, which was delivered every day to a designated spot close to your vision quest area. I had been to the area where the vision quest was going to be held several months before the event and was attracted to a particular spot that seemed to resonate with me.

I had a very busy schedule, as I have most of my life, and because of several commitments, it didn't look like I was going to make this vision quest. I had pretty much given up on the idea, when events rapidly unfolded and opened the way for me to attend at the last minute. I rushed several hundred miles to the event and got there just in time to register at the last minute. All the sites for the vision quest were taken but one, as I was the last person to fill the last spot available for the course. The last spot available was the one that I'd had the connection with! I've come to believe that synchronistic events that unfold in this way are major indicators that you are following in your life's plan and true destiny. That day and into the night we went over what we should expect and how the vision quest worked. During this vision quest, we would stay in a small area and mainly meditate over the four-day period. The only thing we would consume was water; no food was eaten.

I had meditated in different formats over the years, and the longest I had ever remained in meditation was maybe two hours. Now I was going to meditate for four days and nights. I had fasted a few times for a twenty-four-hour period, but this was going to be four days, or ninety-six hours total, so I was going to be in for a very interesting time.

We were told that often the answers that you are searching for come to you immediately, and the rest of the time is spent just with you and spirit. I had read of many masters that had fasted for long periods of time. Buddha was known to have fasted often and for long periods, and Moses and Yeshua both fasted for forty days and nights; many people in several different religions practice fasting as a way to achieve enlightenment.

On the morning of the first day, as I was contemplating the

questions I had for my vision quest, they all unfolded to me clear as day, in rapid succession. I was quite startled because I usually contemplate complex problems in my life for days, weeks, months, and sometimes years before I get a clear answer. I had just had multiple questions answered in a matter of minutes. I had expected to practice meditation on these issues for at least a couple of days, but here they were all laid out. I got that now that the small stuff was out of the way we could move on to some serious work. *Wow!* I thought to myself, *if those questions I have been searching for answers to most of my life are the small stuff, what am I in for?* That answer would come quickly and in a very big way.

Native Americans call the ego "the seducer," the little voice that corrupts and leads one astray. The vision quest is a tool that's used to transcend the power of the ego and gain one's rightful role as the master of self. I would find that fasting would indeed teach me to master my ego. Your ego always wants physical comfort and for life to be easy and expects others to serve it, no matter how inconvenient or humiliating to another. Fasting teaches you to transcend this selfish monster and learn humility and control over your body. I had learned to control my body as a Navy SEAL, getting into freezing cold water, pushing myself to impossible physical limits, and enduring long hours with little to no sleep, but fasting, sitting in one spot for days and overcoming the internal voice of the ego, would be one of the greatest challenges of my life up to this point.

After the first day, my ego was incredulous that I was putting myself through this self- induced torture. It tried every trick to get me to give up. The thoughts in my head were, *Why don't you quit and go home and get some food and rest on a comfortable bed? You've already gotten the answers you came for, so let's go.*

Quieting the voice of the ego takes incredible discipline and patience. After the second day, the voice slowed down. I was no longer hungry to the point where I thought I was going to die, which was a trick the ego was trying to get me to believe. On the third day, everything was quiet in my mind; the little death had happened, and now I was prepared for the real work. I was relaxed and peaceful. It was one of the best feelings and the worst feelings I'd had in my life, because as the peaceful feelings washed over me, I began to see all of the negative events that the little voice had caused me in my life. I would focus on these thoughts and the feelings that they caused within me, and then I learned to let them go. It was a wonderful feeling to let go of things within me that I had no idea that I had been holding onto. The memories would flood through me like a wave from a dam that had just burst. As I let them go, the peaceful feeling would return and wash over me. I would be in bliss for a time, and then another painful memory would arise from seemingly nowhere and I would repeat the painful process until it was all done. Tears of sorrow and frustration would sting my eyes, sometimes gasps of pain would wrack my body, and then it would be over as quickly as it came. Just when I thought I could bear no more, I would get release, and the blissful ecstasy would return, and the tears of pain would be replaced with tears of joy.

I remember going through a whole day like this on the third day when I had the emotional cleansing roller coaster. I was grateful for the experience, and now I knew what the real work was all about that my spirit had planned for me. I watched the sun go down and listened to the chorus of the birds as the night approached, peaceful and content. The stars came out, and I felt the immense expanse of the cosmos and felt myself expand. I felt a oneness with all of life as never before. The spot that I had picked out was interesting in that it was under the largest tree in the area. The unique thing about it was that it was no longer alive. It was still standing strong, with outstretched branches supporting an amazing number of birds during the morning and evening chorus, but it was no longer a living part of the lush forest that surrounded me. The many different colorful birds that perched on its branches, as they had for hundreds of years, were perched on a slowly disintegrating, once living entity. It was symbolic of what I was experiencing: the little death of the ego and the return to oneness with all life.

I heard a whippoorwill begin to call out in the darkness. You will only hear a whippoorwill at night, and you will rarely if ever see one. I had heard that a whippoorwill's call is the saddest call in the night, because it is calling for a mate. It is searching for happiness. Since I was a little boy, I had always wanted to see a whippoorwill. I had often tried to follow its call so that I could get a glimpse of one, but it would just distance itself from me, still calling. No matter how stealthy and quiet I was, it would still slip away from me as if it sensed rather than heard or saw me. Before the first light of the dawn, the searching calls would seem to fade away, and you wouldn't hear it again until it was completely dark the next night. I felt myself drift off, staring through the branches of the dead tree at the night sky with the stars winking at me in the heavens and drifted off to sleep, listening to the sounds of the whippoorwill's call.

My sleep was filled with dreams of the same process that I had gone through during the day. Frustrating scenes of my life interspersed with dreams of bliss. I heard a loud, annoying sound in my dream, and I came half out of my dream with the intent to stop the noise so that I could try and sleep soundly. I looked up, half in, half out of sleep and saw a whippoorwill staring down at me. It made its call again, and it seemed deafening to me. I was irritated and half sat up and shooed it away and then lay back down again. My eyes shot back open immediately, and I sat back up with the sudden realization that one of my lifelong dreams was sitting right above me, almost close enough to touch. The whippoorwill was gone as if by magic. I couldn't believe it! It was so fleeting, a booming sound, a quick look, and then a dream of mine for so long had gone. I lay back down and pondered the irony of it. The night was quiet and then, off in the distance, was the sound of a whippoorwill, possibly never to be seen again in my lifetime. I drifted back off to sleep.

The next day, I awoke before the chorus of the birds and went out to the spot on the trail where I would get my gallon of water for the day. If I left an empty gallon the morning before, then a new, full one would be waiting for me. I put another stick in the ground by my pick up point to mark my fourth and last day, and then went silently back to my quest spot. I watched the sun rise as the birds sang, and then as it traveled higher into the sky, it became quiet again. I sat in anticipation of more emotional roller-coaster rides, but nothing came. I sat in silence with barely a thought crossing my mind. Time became fluid, and I thought of a Salvador Dali museum I had gone to in St. Petersburg, Florida, while I was in the area during time off between training missions in the SEAL teams. Dali painted clocks and watches in surrealist paintings that appeared to be melting, almost formless and flowing over his canvases with out-of-place scenes of nature or abstract characters. I felt like time was formless for me now. The day drifted by slowly, almost imperceptibly, as I sat in silence and just quietly witnessed it, with barely a thought. The little death was complete, and now I would be the witness of my life and not my ego. It was like being in heaven on earth. The day flowed into night, and with the whippoorwill's lonesome song, I drifted off into a deep and peaceful sleep.

After I awoke early the next morning, it was time to go back down to the campsite where I would review and write down what had transpired during my four days of questing. I quietly gathered my few things and looked around at the setting of my first vision quest, taking in the scene for the last time, expressing my gratitude for the incredible gift I had been given, and then I silently walked out.

I was deeply humbled and moved on an inner level by my experience, which I could not have comprehended before this moment in time. One of the things I wanted to continue to work on was learning to be humble in all things. It's not an easy task, and it continues to challenge me because just when I think I've got it all figured out, it's about time to be humbled again.

One of the greatest lessons that humanity could learn is that we are not our egos; our egos are part of us, but they should never rule us as they do most of humanity. We can and should be the masters of our egos and not the other way around. If I had not learned how to gain control of my ego, I would never have advanced to the level of awareness and intuitional abilities that I would experience in the future.

As I continued down the trail to the camp, I thought back to that young American Indian BUD/S trainee that had inspired me to do a vision quest like he had mentioned in his letter to his grandfather during Hell Week many years ago. and said a silent thank-you.

"WE CAN EASILY FORGIVE A CHILD WHO IS AFRAID OF THE DARK; THE REAL TRAGEDY OF LIFE IS WHEN MEN ARE AFRAID OF THE LIGHT."

◊ *Plato* ◊

Chapter 14

ANCIENT KNOWLEDGE

While traveling throughout the world, I have come across many ancient sites where civilizations have come and gone. I have wondered at how these magnificent temples and cities could have been built at times when man was supposed to be primitive and incapable of the advanced technological skills necessary for building some of these incredible architectural achievements that could not be replicated today. Let's just take one amazing achievement that was used in the building of the great pyramids in Giza for example. The mortar that was used to join the massive blocks of limestone weighing between two and seventy tons each is of an unknown origin. The chemical composition is known and has been analyzed but cannot be replicated using current technology. This is just one of thousands of technological anomalies that exist throughout the world that ancient cultures should not have been capable of achieving if we blindly believe in the hypotheses of today's academic teachings, which argue that we have had a consistent and unbroken advancement, or gradualism, from primitive Paleolithic man to today's man. Do we just shrug our shoulders and continue to say "we don't know how it happened but since they were primitive people they don't count?" Many of ancient man's achievements cannot be replicated today, even with our current technology, such as the movement, shaping, and placement of megalithic stones throughout the world. Megalithic stones are to be found throughout the world in places like Machu Picchu and Sacsayhuaman Temple in Peru, The Valley Temple of the Giza Plateau and the Osireion of Abydos in Egypt, Stonehenge and Ashbury Circle in England, and the Temple of Bacchus in Baalbek, Lebanon, which has a stone block that is estimated to weigh 350 tons (or 772,000 pounds) next to the Roman Temple that was built on top of the ancient megalithic stones. In the quarry three miles away is a stone that was quarried but not yet moved that weighed 1500 tons. All of these stones were so precisely shaped and fitted together that you cannot slide a razor blade between them. I have seen all of the above except the Temple of Bacchus, and it is evident as you stand in awe of these megaliths that a very advanced race had a hand in their construction.

If we take into account that earth has naturally undergone sudden, radical, violent, worldwide geological events, or catastrophism, throughout its history, as was the accepted thought throughout most of man's history on earth, then we can begin to account for these mysteries among us.

If we give credence to the universality of the deluge stories throughout the world, we get a view of human history that records stories similar to the one in the Christian Bible. The story of Noah and the flood that covered the earth is an historic event that is similar to other cultures and countries such as the Babylonian, Sumerian, Jewish, Islamic, Indian, Chinese, Laotian, Australian, Polynesian, Germanic, Irish, and, in the Americas, the Aztec, Incan, Mayan, and Hopi. There are several others I have not named because they are too numerous to list them all, but I think you probably get the picture.

Man has risen to great heights of achievement and then a catastrophic event has struck the earth and wiped out all progress, sending man back to the proverbial Stone Age to rebuild amongst the ruins, until most, if not all, memory is lost or covered up and disregarded because it does not fit the prevailing paradigm.

We are constantly being given new information to support this event in our history. Recently, it was reported that tropical coral has been found in Antarctica, that large groups of woolly mammoths have been found with their giant hip bones smashed as if hit by a giant tidal wave that rushed across a lush tundra of ancient northern Siberia. This mostly frozen and barren area once supported their need for copious amounts of vegetative matter. They were then flash frozen until over ten thousand years later, as the ice sheet that had frozen them in time near the Arctic Circle began to retreat. Even the buttercup vegetation that they had been grazing on was found undigested in their stomachs, also indicating that they had been greatly traumatized and then frozen within hours. The vegetation found in their stomachs no longer grows in this area and cannot be found until you travel over a thousand miles away to warmer climates in the south. This all indicates a rapid shift in the location of the arctic pole to the current location just north of their remains.

In the book *Maps of the Ancient Sea Kings: Evidence of Advanced Civilization in the Ice Age* by Charles H. Hapgood, he discusses ancient maps that came into the hands of an admiral of the Turkish Navy named Piri Re'is in the year 1513. The map gives the coastal outline of Antarctica without ice sheeting! This is intriguing because scientists estimate that Antarctica has been covered by ice up to two miles thick in some places for at least ten thousand years. This area of the world was first mapped by seismic profile in 1949. Hapgood speculated that the earth's crust has shifted many times throughout Earth's history, sending the poles to new locations and causing worldwide disastrous results. Albert Einstein, who believed in catastrophism, studied Hapgood's work and agreed with it. It is currently estimated that Earth has undergone fourteen magnetic reversals in the last four and a half million years.

Most geologists today believe in both catastrophism and uniformitarianism alike, taking the viewpoint that our planet's geological formation is gradual, with occasional shattering events that have affected Earth and its inhabitants. The mass extension of the dinosaurs is an example of millions of years of gradual evolution virtually wiped out by a catastrophic event. Another recent example occurred from July 16 through July 22, 1994, when pieces of the comet Shoemaker-Levy 9 collided with Jupiter, creating a spectacular demonstration of a natural catastrophic event for all to witness.

If we accept that cataclysmic moments have occurred in our history, then we begin to see that it is plausible that advanced civilizations could have existed in Earth's history as well. A civilization with advanced mapping skills and the ability to see the earth from above was indicated in the Peri Re'is maps. Not only was Antarctica mapped, but many other regions on Earth were mapped long before they were discovered. For example, the Americas were mapped long before Columbus sailed across the Atlantic Ocean to *rediscover* them. Stories of ancient advanced civilizations as described by Plato in the dialogues of Timaeus and Critias give an account of a legendary island called Atlantis that sank into the ocean "in a single day and night of misfortune." Detailed descriptions of the land, people, customs, architecture, and history are covered. Many cultures today claim to be descendants of the people of Atlantis; among them are the Mayans of Mexico, who openly state that they are of Atlantian descent.

The Polynesians of Micronesia claim they are descendants of a lost continent of Lemuria, which sank during the same catastrophic event that sank Atlantis and inspired cultures around the world with deluge stories. These advanced cultures have left their mark upon our consciousness, as we are fascinated with the mysterious structures that have survived cataclysmic events. Hollywood has sparked our awareness of the possibility of a worldwide end to civilization as we know it with movies like *Armageddon* and *The Day the Earth Stood Still*. We are enthralled with ancient prophecies and try to understand the shrouded messages from the past they have left for us.

What, if anything, can ancient cultures have left us that we can utilize today in our seemingly advanced culture? What information from the past that appears to be focused on the mystical and spiritual aspects, versus the materialistic and strictly analytical aspects of man, can possibly influence us or give us a message about upcoming changes in the planet? Are we ready to unlock their secrets, or do we continue to dismiss their mysteries as mere myths and legends from a bygone age that has no relation to our new and evolved civilization?

The ancient Maya of Mexico created cosmic calendars capable of describing the evolutionary cycles of our Milky Way galaxy. A large 1300-year-old stelae carved in Coba, Mexico, mathematically charts the Earth's cycles from the "big bang" of 16.5 billion years ago all the way up to 2012, where it ends. Modern scientists have agreed upon many of the evolutionary milestones and dates outlined in the stelae. Barbara Hand Clow in her book *The Mayan Code* gives an excellent argument for the Mayans to have left us a calendar that points to major shifts in consciousness and the advancement of the earth. The Mayans appear to have known more about the galaxy than we currently know and left us a message in their calendar that we are nearing the end of time, as we have known it. We are about to be ushered into a golden age in the next few years that will transform us. Many people are starting to awaken to their intuitional capabilities as I have discussed throughout this book, and the Mayans and many ancient cultures knew it would happen thousands of years ago.

The earth revolves around the sun, and as it does so it has a slight wobble like a spinning top that changes the relationship of the winter equinox as it rises at designated points on the horizon. Every 71.6 years, the precessional cycle of the equinox moves this point on the ecliptic one degree, so that after 2,147.6 years, it moves through one constellation of the zodiac. After 25,771.5 years, we complete a cycle through all the celestial zodiacal signs. We are currently moving from Pisces into Aquarius. If we turn the clock back to 10,500 BC, we would be in the constellation of Leo, and if we look at where the Sphinx of Giza is facing it would correlate with this point in time. All over the planet are ancient sites, temples, and monuments that are positioned to align with star systems, like the pyramids of Giza which are aligned with the stars of Sirius of Orion's belt. The Dogon tribe of Africa, believed to be of Egyptian descent, traces their astronomical lore back to 3200 BC. According to Dogon traditions, the star Sirius has a companion star, which is invisible to the human eye, and French anthropologists recorded this belief in the 1930s. The star, which scientists today call Sirius B, was not discovered until 1970 by a large telescope. There are hundreds of similar examples of advanced astronomical knowledge throughout the world, which point to advanced cultures in past ages. We have, regrettably, slowly let this knowledge slip away or suppressed or destroyed it through our callous need to control our world so that we can forget the painful past.

The Mayans were deeply connected with the cyclic patterns of the heavens and how they affected the earth. Every equinox (March 21 and September 22), the Pyramid of Kukulcan in Chichén Itzá in the Yucatán peninsula of Mexico has the visibly undulating pattern of a snake, caused by the late afternoon angle of the sun that links up with a carved stone serpent's head at the bottom of the structure. The Mayans saw the snake as a representation of the Milky Way and calculated long ago a point in the heavens where we will line up with the center of the galaxy. That point in time is the winter solstice of 21 December 2012, when the earth aligns with the galactic center and its anticenter region of the Pleiades. In the book *Galactic Alignment*, John Major Jenkins points out that this is an extremely rare occurrence and the Maya believed it would stimulate consciousness in a profound way.

I believe that major changes are underway that will revolutionize the way our economic and political systems operate; I also believe that our consciousness and the way we interact with each other and the planet will have a direct bearing on how future earth changes transpire. The Harmonic Convergence of August 16 and 17 in 1987 is an example of a large portion of the planet coming together to focus their intent on a positive outcome for humanity. The Convergence was an announcement of the forthcoming end of time and a preparation to move from third dimensional reality into fourth dimensional reality of time. For the Mayan calendar, a great cycle ended and a new one commenced.

According to the Mayans, it is time that holds the universe

together, and not gravity. Time is the mathematics of the universal laws of nature, the unifying force that holds everything together. During the height of classic Mayan civilization lived a leader named Pacal Votan who ruled in what is present day Chiapas, Mexico. He is credited with inscribing stone monuments with precise astronomical and astrological information. Pacal Votan's sentiment was "All is number. God is a number. God is in all." We are intimately linked and formed by the galaxy. All of life is ordered by the same basic, reoccurring patterns. The Harmonic Convergence was the ending of the mechanical time measurement of 12:60 (twelve months in a year, sixty minutes in an hour) and the beginning of the natural frequency of time of 13:20, upon which the Mayan calendar is based. Natural time contains thirteen moons of twenty-eight days each and one day for reflection and forgiveness. Twenty is the number of totality. You have twenty digits (fingers and toes) because God has made you the totality of time. Thirteen is the number of God's cosmic wisdom, perfect in its power of unceasing change and circulation. Thirteen are the major joints of your limbs and body, which are the ankles, knees, hips, wrists, elbows, shoulders and neck.

We are tied to each other, the earth and our galaxy. Our thoughts and actions can and will create our environment and our new world. Ancient wisdom was passed down to use from many sources all over the earth. They all point to a time in the near future that they said would change us and our world as we know it. We have become our own masters in many ways, and I believe we will learn to master the new energies from the galactic core as we again come under their influence after our twelve-thousand-year journey through space, away from the galactic core's positive influences. The Mayans said time as we know it will end on December 21, 2012. It will not be the end for us as a species, as many are saying, but for the mathematical way we use time, as Gregg Braden explains in *Fractal Time: The Secret of 2012 and a New World Age*. As the emerging energies begin to gather momentum and come strongly into the earth, they will influence our world in a way of our choosing, through our thoughts and intuition.

"MOST PEOPLE TREAT THE PRESENT MOMENT AS IF IT WERE AN OBSTACLE THAT THEY NEED TO OVERCOME. SINCE THE PRESENT MOMENT IS LIFE ITSELF, IT IS AN INSANE WAY TO LIVE."

◊ *Eckhart Tolle* ◊

Chapter 15

FULL CIRCLE

I often wondered as a child and as a young man how some things seemed to come to me naturally, while other things were difficult. For instance, I found the study of different ancient philosophies intriguing and easy to grasp, while other philosophies, like religion, were sometimes beautiful and captivating and at other times strange and incomprehensible. I would find school mostly uninspiring and dry, but when I studied the same information on my own, it was amazing and powerful. There were times when I would be asking questions that stumped my teachers to the point where my classmates would jokingly ask me to get up and teach the course. I remember reading once how an author had questioned how on earth such fascinating subjects could be made so boring by the educational system. I did of course have a few gifted teachers who would challenge me in a positive way, and I would excel in their subjects to a great level. These gifted teachers unfortunately were few and far between. Sports were a favorite pastime of mine, and at one time I fancied myself getting a college scholarship, but I just couldn't see myself doing the horribly boring schoolwork. It was off to the military for me, because I knew deep down it was my calling.

I ask myself at times what brought me to this point and why I do the things that I do. I have found that human beings have a proclivity for certain things because of the level of ability that we pushed ourselves to in previous lives. These things come naturally and easily because we have had many lives in which to perfect them.

I believe we come into incarnation to advance ourselves in certain areas, and if we start down a path that is contrary to what our plan is, then we will find it boring and eventually drift away from it. If we are really drawn to something, but it is really difficult, it is perhaps because we have not had experience in this area but are attracted to it because it is part of our life's purpose or plan. I have learned the hard way that when doors keep slamming shut in your face, you need to find the doors that open easily and invite you in. Part of my life was in search of these doors, and it is quite exciting when you finally find the ones that are just right for you.

Some people believe that our lives are unchangeably mapped out already or controlled by unseen forces. I do not adhere to this belief, but am convinced that we have free will and can either continue on the path that we have mapped out before we incarnated or can take a separate trail. There are many paths to enlightenment, and the one we take is completely unique to us as individuals, but they all lead ultimately to the same place. We are all on our paths to "at-one- ment" with the divine and sometimes we move along as a group and at times we may decide to travel alone.

I have found as my intuition has developed that I have memories of the times that I have lived and that certain lives are coming forward stronger than others at this time. I have had many military incarnations in my history as a soul on this earth, in different armies all over the world. I have incarnated as warriors, warrior-kings, high-ranking officers, soldiers, and sailors. I have fought and died in countless historic battles throughout the ages.

Many other incarnations have been as high-ranking priests and shamans to simple monks in religions all over the world that have come and gone and in some that still exist. I can remember many of these places, and I'm drawn to them like someone who has been away from their beloved home for a long time and wishes to return.

Because of my personal history, the martial world comes naturally and easily to me, as do philosophy and spirituality. Both of these disciplines are almost second nature for me, and it's no surprise to me that I've lived and died by the sword and been a man of the cloth as well, many times in many lives, as related by several psychics.

My intuitional abilities have come through as the result of the development from these many lives. All of my many incarnations have intertwined and prepared me up to this point in my life. This book is the fruition of many lives, and many masters' work, both military and spiritual, that have taught me the wisdom and discipline to master my own life and pass this information on to humanity.

Although I have studied with many noteworthy masters throughout time, the one that stands out the most against the backdrop of history is Yeshua ben Joseph or Jesus. He was one of my master teachers that I feel is impacting me the most in this life. His message of love and the awakening of intuition are coming through me in a multitude of ways. My life plan that I have been drawn to and as has been relayed to me through psychics is to teach the art of intuition.

Newtonian physics explains our three dimensional world, and now with quantum physics we have the science of the fourth and fifth dimensional world. These dimensions are stacked, or overlaid, one over the other, and impact our three-dimensional world in ways we are just beginning to realize. As we accept the possibility of time being nonlinear in different dimensions, we can see that time—past, present, and future—is happening simultaneously and impacting our now. I relate accepting this as a valid concept to our belief just a few hundred years ago that the earth was flat and was the center of the universe.

Ancient cultures had an understanding of this concept of time, but because it didn't fit the prevailing power's ideas, it was suppressed and eventually forgotten except by a secret few. Personally, I have felt that secret societies that have this wonderfully enlightening information should come forward and share it. I see from the past, though, that if you came forward with information that is contrary to the established powers that be, there could be severe consequences. Surely that's not the case now, is it? Perhaps a level of awareness must first be attained to bring forth this valuable insight, and the holders of this information are waiting until they see this event happen in humanity. I have found that the information is mostly there, but you must search for it and piece it together.

Awareness must be established before you can begin to see things and understand their impact. For instance, on an intellectual basis I understood the earth was not flat and that it revolved around the sun. But it was not until I saw the Apollo moon landings with the astronauts looking back and videoing the earth that I started to become aware of these teachings from school as accurate. On a deeper level, it was not until as a young man, when I became a sailor on the open seas and started making long overseas air-flights, that I became fully aware of the curvature of the earth and its position in space. I look forward to the next level of awareness when someday space travel will be available to the average person.

So stretching our awareness is often done in increments, or, unfortunately, in the case of those few individuals that still cling to the concept that the earth is flat, not at all. This understanding of different dimensions is not mandatory to be intuitional; it just helps those of us who like to see a rational side to things as well as the non-rational. We live in a world where both rational and non-rational realities exist side by side, but if you cling too tightly to one or the other, you become disconnected with a larger and deliciously exciting world.

Brian L. Weiss, MD, reveals in his book *Same Soul, Many Bodies* how past and present lives can affect our future lives, and how our future lives can transform us in the here and now. I have read many books by this revolutionary author, and have found they have opened my awareness to alternate realities that I have come to accept as part of my own.

Toward the end of my career as a SEAL, around the twenty-year mark, I noticed that my intuition was awakening in a major way. By the time I got to the twenty-four-year mark, I had made plans to get out and teach what I had learned in the SEAL teams to the public. Once I got out of the Navy, I began teaching a variety of courses combining my Special Forces skills with my awakened intuition skills. I found that people with no military experience were grasping the concepts and skills that I was teaching very rapidly. I ran a Hell Week course that taught the students how to tap into the intuitive brain wave patterns. This knowledge would allow them to do the incredible levels of physical endurance that I had planned for them that was in some ways even more advanced than BUD/S training. It was an incredible affirmation that teaching intuitive skills from the beginning could not only increase performance levels, but also drastically shorten the time needed for training.

I later started security contracting, and that was where my intuition skills really accelerated and blossomed into several other skills previously unknown to me. I'm now fully conscious that I've developed into an intuitive warrior. With the realization of this knowledge, my desire now is to pass this information on to humanity.

"ALL THAT WE ARE IS THE RESULT OF WHAT WE HAVE THOUGHT. THE MIND IS EVERYTHING. WHAT WE THINK, WE BECOME."

◊ *Buddha* ◊

Chapter 16

THE LAW OF ATTRACTION

I began to understand the concept that "we are what we think most about" around midway through my career as a Navy SEAL at SEAL Team Six, the tier-one antiterrorist team. Whenever I would focus on doing room clearance in my mind before I entered a room, I would picture myself aggressively entering the room and shooting the bad guy targets, or Tangos (for Terrorists) as we called them, and not shooting the Hostages, or Hotels. It was always a game for us to try and set up rooms that were challenging and would push the operators entering the room to the point where they might possibly shoot a hostage if they were not completely focused. The offending operator who shot the hostage had to buy a case of beer for our assault team's beer mess. I had issued myself a challenge to not shoot any hostages for a year. I had already bought my share of beer for the first year I was on the assault team, like most guys, and I was committed to not shooting a single Hotel, and to shooting the Tango targets as rapidly as possible so that they would not have a chance to shoot back or shoot one of my teammates. So I determined through much introspection that I needed to change the way I thought before I entered the room. I really enjoyed being the first in the room because if the number one man entered the room with explosive force and speed, then it set the stage for the rest of the team and helped to contribute to the possibility of success for the rest of the operation. I remember coiling up at the door, ready to enter after having entered hundreds of rooms up to this point in my career, but this time I had determined to use self-talk that quieted my mind with the thought that no matter what scenario played out in the room, I would handle it in the most perfect manner possible. I would be calm internally, but to look at me you would think I was ready to explode with energy—which I was, but in a focused manner that was far more effective in moving into the rooms, intuitively acquiring targets, and getting shots off faster and more accurately than ever, because I learned to quiet my mind and think positive thoughts.

"As you sow, so shall you reap" is a phrase that agrarian societies could comprehend and which fit that age perfectly. The same words rephrased in information age terminology could possibly be "garbage in, garbage out," referring to computer programming but also to our minds, which are in some respects similar to a computer. I have pasted together several different terms that seem to transcend all ages that I try and live by and that are expressions of the idea that whatever you think or dwell upon, whether positive or negative, that is what will ultimately manifest in your life.

If you are going to progress in consciousness, you have to effect change. If you are going to evolve your creative energy in this reality, then you must have an awakening to the possibility that your thoughts will affect your environment by attracting to you what you most think about. You must be able to control your thoughts and intuitively focus on positive outcomes. Whenever a negative thought intrudes, you must learn to replace it with a positive one or you will be trapped in creating a negative reality for yourself and those around you.

We are all master creators, and we create our world through our thoughts. At this very moment, you are a culmination of the thoughts you have had. Take responsibility for your life and think the thoughts that you would have happen in your life. If you want to lose weight, for example, do you think about how fat you are? If so, you will stay that way. You must think of the desired weight or look you wish to have and think only of that. If your self-talk is "I do not wish to be fat" or you look in the mirror and say to yourself that you are fat, then your subconscious is going to hear "I wish to be fat," because it doesn't hear want or not want, it just hears whatever it is that you are focused on. Focus your thoughts on exclusively what you want. A better way to self-talk is "everything I do throughout the day leads me intuitively to my desired figure." Then you see in your mind your desired figure. If you find yourself slipping, then refocus your thoughts again until your thoughts are always positive. You will eventually intuit that you are actually doing the right things that will help you achieve your desired outcome. The more positive thoughts you have and the more desire you put into getting what you want, the closer what you desire will come to you, until one day you wake up with the figure you have focused on.

I have read many books on this subject, and one of the best in my opinion is *The Law of Attraction: The Basics of the Teachings of Abraham*, by Esther and Jerry Hicks. You must become a student of positive information and surround yourself with people of like mind. My wife, children, and I attended an Alaskan cruise with Esther and Jerry to further our understanding of this information. They delved deeply into the Law of Attraction, and the conference room on the cruise ship was filled with lawyers, doctors, actors and actresses, and people of every conceivable walk of life, intently listening to the lectures. We would often see a famous actress in the concierge room where we got coffee and snacks, so it was encouraging to see that these valuable ideas are transcending all areas of humanity.

Over the years, I've worked with several people who were full of bravado and talked about how they wanted to take on the enemy and show them a thing or two. Much of this is forced bravado from guys who are trying to present an image that is not a reality for them, and they hide behind a façade of strength, when in reality they are scared stiff. Another thing that promotes this false bravado is many training institutions, military included, which are trying to mill out people who will pull a trigger if told to, but who don't really have the proper internal training to deal with the stress that is associated with combat operations. After being in designated combat areas in several places in the world for over six years straight now, I can tell you that most of those guys with false bravado have either changed their tune or they are no longer around. Some of them have attracted the combat that they wanted and died, others have been exposed for what they were and have been slowly screened out of the system, and still others have gotten smart and stopped talking about attracting a negative situation. I have been in groups over the last several years in which we all intuitively thought pretty much the same about how talk about bringing on the fighting was not a good idea. We let guys know immediately that if they start their foolish banter about getting some combat action, then they were going to attract it to the group, and we wanted no part of that. If it comes, we will handle it in an expeditious and effective manner, but we have seen and heard too many stories about guys talking smack about getting into a firefight to know that kind of talk will invariably attract it.

One of the best accounts to illustrate this point is a song by Johnnie Cash called "Ring of Fire." The Law of Attraction works in interesting ways, and this account is no exception. Some of the guys in a protection detail that I work with on occasion were riding down a road in Afghanistan playing the song "Ring of Fire" when a roadside bomb went off and decimated the armored car they were in. Fortunately, they all survived with minor cuts and bruises. They were able to save the CD, which continued to play until they ejected it, but the car was totaled. Several days later, they learned from friends in Iraq that roadside bombs had destroyed several military vehicles in Iraq during the last few months while playing that same song. As a joke, the protective detail team put a warning label on the CD that said, "Do not play while operating a motor vehicle."

My father listened to country music, and growing up I heard Johnny Cash songs on occasion and enjoyed his music. Mr. Cash had a colorful life and played in his early days as a singer and songwriter with one of my favorites at the time, Elvis Presley. Johnny had some hard times when depression and drug addiction almost ruined his career and his life. I believe it's possible that this time in his life may have unfortunately influenced his music during this dark period. While writing this story, I decided to do a little research to see if I could find more information on "Ring of Fire." I was quite surprised by what I found, but I probably shouldn't have been. To add even more emphasis to how words affect our environment and attract to us not only what we say and think, but also what we hear is the fact that the house Cash shared with his wife June burned down in a "ring of fire" in April 2007, around the same time my friends had their car decimated by a roadside bomb while listening to his song.

As a young boy, I remember loving science to the point where I would really apply myself with great enthusiasm to my studies and in class. I had just moved to a grade level where they actually gave you "A-F" grades instead of satisfactory or unsatisfactory. I came home one afternoon and excitedly told my parents that I believed I was going to get an "A plus" in science. My parents both said, "That is not likely as an A plus is a very advanced grade." I was crushed, but still believed I'd get that grade. When I did, it was even more of a letdown when they still weren't impressed and merely said, "You probably won't be able to maintain it." I later learned that both my parents had not done well in school and believed that I was destined for the same.

I have traveled throughout most of the world by now, and after over thirty years of almost continuous travel, I can see the effect that this attitude of passing on the failings of the parents is having on the world. Your environment does have an effect on you, and if you are in a negative place and don't rise above it, you will be repeating the same pattern. In the Middle East, the negative vibrations of war have been repeating themselves for thousands of years. This dark energy vortex is a problem that is drawing the world into its madness repeatedly and will continue until the people in this area are taught how to pull themselves out of the negative vibrations they are caught in.

Generation after generation is taught hatred for their neighbors that transcends all dealings with any group outside of their tribe, religious sect, or even immediate family. Nearly every religion on earth today teaches love, peace, and forgiveness, yet it is thought that if someone wrongs you, then you are justified in retaliating, even if it goes against the teachings of the particular religion.

I've worked with many Middle Eastern countries' Special Forces over the years and always had a good rapport with them. We would bring them to our training facilities in the States, and they would have open access to train as we did. I was amazed at the depth of their ability to not practice forgiveness and to hold onto negativity. This thought pattern was brought into sharp focus for me when a platoon of SEALs I was in deployed for six months to the Middle East. We were excited to travel to this one country because they had a shooting house that we would be able to train in and keep up our skills. This shoot house had been designed, built, and paid for by the U.S. military, or the American taxpayer if you get down to the bottom line of where the money came from. We were shocked to learn that we would not be allowed to either train them in it or to have access to it ourselves because a platoon of SEALs over a year and a half ago had used "their" facility (it was on their land after all), and had not cleaned up after themselves. No amount of reasoning would convince them to let us use it. After all that had been done for and with them, and promises of more to follow, they still would not change their minds. We had not even performed this perceived insult to them, yet we were being made to pay for it. The platoon that committed the perceived injustice was probably not even aware that they had done anything wrong. I remember having to clean a barracks facility that these same guys had used after they had left it a mess in the U.S.

You don't get mad at this ingrained and defective thought pattern and you don't plan to get even, because that would pull you into the same negative vortex. The best thing that we found to do was to focus on being professional and set an example that would be an inspiration for them in the future. I'm not giving this example to assign blame and finger-pointing. No one is perfect, and we learn from each other in various and sundry ways. I see my brothers and sisters in the Middle East as equals, and I want the best for them as I do for my own family.

There appears to me to be an incarnate pattern of anger and hatred, which are manifestations of fear, and which is repeating and creating a vortex of darkness. This constantly revolving circle of despondency is sucking the life out of the people in the Middle East. To turn this energy pattern around will take the knowledge of what is really transpiring, and that is that fear is the predominant energy, and it needs to be replaced with the energy of love.

The first step should be to bring the people who are growing up in families filled with unconscious hatred around to the awareness that they are fomenting and fostering patterns of darkness. I believe this would be the first step toward turning this area around.

The second step would be to replace the pattern of fear with love. This is not an easy task, and will take the leaders of all aspects of society, from government to education to religion, to replace the pervasive fear with love. The energy pattern of love and light will replace those of fear and darkness when allowed, but the cycle of fear must be broken first.

The third and last step would be for the world to recognize their plight and encourage them to excel at moving away from darkness and into the light, a process that has begun and should be recognized.

The Law of Attraction is a powerful tool for accessing your intuition when you fully understand how it works and believe in its ability to transform your life. When using the Law of Attraction, always focus on the inner heart space, which is the most powerful place in the universe, because there you are one with God and are your most effective at creating.

"WE SUCCEED ONLY AS WE IDENTIFY IN LIFE, OR IN WAR, OR IN ANYTHING ELSE, A SINGLE OVERRIDING OBJECTIVE, AND MAKE ALL OTHER CONSIDERATIONS BEND TO THAT ONE OBJECTIVE."

◊ *Dwight D. Eisenhower* ◊

Chapter 17

SUCCESS OR FAILURE THROUGH WORDS

I observed early on as a SEAL that if I focused on success, then I would invariably achieve it. The same was true for failure. Whatever the mind is focused on, that is what is attracted. If I were to brief an operation or training event, I would be careful to focus on the words that I used and make sure they were positive and relayed how I was interested in the final outcome as the success for the operation. The process, which we later honed to teach the hand-to-hand course incorporated this knowledge and is called Neuro-linguistic Programming or NLP for short. It describes how words (linguistics) affect our minds (neurology) and how we program ourselves, either consciously or subconsciously, for success or failure through self-talk or verbalized words that are incorporated into our minds. I was not interested in every micromanaged detail being achieved, as many of my commanders seemed to be. I knew that what was briefed as far as the route taken to and from the target and actions at the objective was just a guideline and should never, if deviated from, constitute a failure of the mission. I trusted in the teamwork, training, and creative ingenuity of those I briefed or of those briefs I listened to and critiqued. I knew that the more positive the brief, the greater the chance for success, and vice versa for a negative brief. No real-world combat operation or training evolution that I was ever part of ever happened as briefed. What would amaze me was that some commanders would get radically upset if briefed operations deviated from what was planned, even if the final objective was successfully reached. Many commanders would negatively critique well thought out briefs to the point where I and many other leaders would brief our guys who were doing the missions that this is the brief for the commanders and afterwards we'll get together and do the brief for what we are actually doing. Lots of time was wasted putting together elaborate briefs that could have been better spent prepping and fine-tuning gear. After getting chewed up in a brief, and having lots of negativity thrown around about how we should have been better prepared, we would go out and try and pump the guys back up so that they didn't go out thinking they were failures from the beginning.

One of the longest mission briefs I can remember attending was a combat operation during Operation Just Cause in Panama, in which we were to raid a house where General Noriega was supposedly held up. The brief went on and on ad nauseam with micromanaged "what ifs" throughout the mission brief. Our mission commander did an amazing job covering an incredible number of contingencies, or "what ifs," but still the top commander wanted to know more: "What if your lead helicopter goes down? What will you do? What if you can't find the house Noriega is in?" It went on and on. I wanted to ask, "What if a bus full of clowns shows up and starts marching up the street we're to set up on?"

Commanders wanted to know if you had thought out as many different contingencies as were likely to occur along your entire operation, and they never seemed to be satisfied. Some commanders would become angry and belittling in their debrief of a mission plan if they felt you hadn't covered some obscure contingency that only they could have thought of. This often doomed a mission before it ever started, because it set up a negative mindset or NLP in the team that they didn't have a good enough brief and would fail because of it. Our missions were so micromanaged at times that some guys wouldn't know what to do if a contingency arose that wasn't covered in the brief. You can never come up with every "what if"; that is impossible because situations are constantly evolving, moment to moment, which can completely change everything. Of course on our way into the target area to capture Noriega, we took a few rounds before we set down the helos, and virtually the entire brief went out the window. If the plan had been rigidly followed, the team would have never made it to the target, because the helos were forced to set down in a completely different area. Fortunately, because of our high level of training, confidence, and teamwork, the team easily adapted and provided a successful mission. If the mission had been judged on the micromanaged points all the way into the target, it would have been judged a failure. But the end point was achieved through the flexibility of the team to constantly adapt to battlefield conditions.

A really bad commander would have been disappointed that this contingency had not been thought of and briefed. Even though the team had adapted and achieved the ultimate objective, the mission would have been criticized and deemed a failure overall because all of the "what ifs" had not been covered.

When we taught our hand-to-hand course, we reinforced the need for positive NLP words that would condition a warrior's mind-set for success at the briefing level and carry over throughout the mission and the return of the team. Achieving the objective was the focus of the mission. We wanted to know a general safe plan with a good chance of success built in, and we expected the operators would carry that plan to its completion and do everything in their power to make it happen.

During our multiple attacker scenarios in the hand-to-hand course, we taught that you can never know what punch or kick another man was going to choose; the important thing was to fight with an attitude of always being offensive and hitting targets. That way, you would be in control of the situation and not be affected by the decisions of others. You didn't wait for a pre- trained kick or punch, because this was impossible to predict.

The same is true for all aspects of life. If we sit around thinking of every contingency, we will never get started. If an unexpected contingency were to arise, and we stopped and went back and tried to think of more contingencies that we could plan for so that we wouldn't be surprised, then we would not get very far, and we would miss our opportunities for success. If we went in thinking of failure or what would happen if we failed (NLP), we would most definitely attract that outcome. It was the law of attraction at work on the battlefield, and we had set it up by negative NLP.

This doesn't mean that all I have to do is think positive thoughts and have people repeat positive words around me. This is important, but just as important is taking action toward a positive outcome. If your training or work is full of negative words, actions, and outcomes, then whenever it's time to actually perform whatever it is you do in life, your chances for a positive outcome are greatly diminished.

I remember many times throughout my career in SEAL training that we were told, "We are going to train this way, but if you go into combat you will do it this way." This was incredibly wrong on many different levels. If you train wrong, you will do wrong if you ever have to go and face the real deal. The way the mind and body work and are conditioned to a given response can't be changed just by a random thought if you have already ingrained a certain muscle and thought response into your consciousness.

You have to train and think as if your training is the real thing, or you will get caught regretting what happens when put into a stressful environment wherein you have to think about what you should do in a given circumstance that is counter to how you trained. You just don't have time to ponder in most combat situations; you must instantly react or you instantly die. Combat is a great teacher, but I don't recommend it.

I remember when I came back to my hometown of Columbia, South Carolina, once to visit family and friends after I had been in the military for a few years. A friend and I were out driving, and having lived in California for a few years, I was used to putting on my seatbelt after getting in the car, which was a requirement for drivers in California. It was not a requirement for drivers in S.C. yet, and my friend looked at me and said that he had put a lot of thought into what might happen if he was about to get into a wreck. He demonstrated to me how he had mastered quickly reaching over and deftly fastening his seatbelt. I contemplated this for a moment, pondering how I could break it to him that I thought this was a plan doomed for future failure, when it popped into my mind to ask him what would happen if someone hit him at an angle from which he couldn't see and react? He thought about this a moment and then buckled his seatbelt and did so every time we got in the car from then on.

Don't kid yourself that you will do the right thing when the pressure is on in an emergency, if you don't think about the scenario as if it is really happening. If you think all it takes to survive when your airplane is doing an emergency landing is sitting and screaming, then you are sadly mistaken. I always pay attention when the airline attendants give the safety briefs, because I want to know what to do and ingrain it my mind; then I let it go. You don't have to dwell on what ifs, because you will adapt as long as you have done the basics in your mind first. That's all it takes. If you want to get it down to a Marine Corps silent drill team precision, then you are going to have to practice a whole lot. But just like all the people who were on the airplane that did an emergency landing on the Hudson on January 15, 2009, you will survive and you will execute correctly if you pay attention like it's the real thing. All those people on the plane listened like their lives depended on it, which they did when their plane went into the water. I'm sure they listened to the instructions very intently on what to do and how to survive.

Words have a powerful effect on our thoughts and our bodies. If we are to program ourselves and others to be at our ultimate best, we must always consider the correct and efficient use of the words we use.

Consider this scenario: a child is running along the top of a wall that is three feet off the ground. You see that there is a potential safety issue, so you shout at the child to be careful or he might fall. The child trips and falls and is hurt. Do you feel vindicated and angry with the child? Suppose the same scenario as above, only you change the words you use to "Great job on balance! Why don't you hop down now and we can go play somewhere else?" The child runs to the end of the wall and hops down without any problems. How do you feel now? Which scenario do you like better? We can always choose to keep our words positive in any scenario, but if we live our lives through fear and ego, then we will always attract to us what we think and say.

Very simply, if we think and speak and act in a negative manner, we will attract that to us. If we think and speak and act in a positive manner, then we will attract that instead. If those around us speak and think and act in a negative or positive manner, then negative or positive things will be attracted to them, and if we are with them, then we will receive what they receive. Although it may be in an indirect manner, we will still be allowing that into our lives. Choose the company you keep wisely.

"A HERO SEEKS AND DEFENDS AT ALL COSTS, KNOWING THAT THE CONSEQUENCE OF DENIAL IS THE TRIUMPH OF EVIL."

◊ *Anonymous* ◊

Chapter 18

TRANSCENDING PAIN AND SUFFERING

Throughout my many trips to different countries around the world, I have noticed a great amount of poverty. I was by no means born with a silver spoon in my mouth, so I have not known great luxuries. I grew up in a lower middle class family, and at times I remember the electricity being turned off by the power company because the bill was late, but at least I had a roof over my head and food to eat. I swam in clear streams, ponds, lakes, and the ocean as a kid. I had safe playgrounds to play on and plenty of friends my age to play with. School was a bore, but at least I had the opportunity for an education. I had toys and books and my own comfortable bed and room. My parents and family loved me, and we always stayed in touch and had family gatherings.

Many people throughout the world live day-to-day, barely surviving. Eighteen thousand children are starving to death every day, based on United Nations' figures. Tragically, I have seen children swimming in polluted waters. Clean drinking water and wells to provide it are scarce in most of the undeveloped world. Mortality rates and life expectancy for much of the earth are dire and getting worse. Most people in the Western world are rarely if ever exposed to this level of poverty, aside from the homeless they occasionally see in big cities, or the slums that they may pass by and try not to look at.

Most of the countries in Central and South America, Asia, Africa, and the Middle East are heavily impoverished. Three billion of the over six and half billion people on earth live on less than two U.S. dollars a day. We are constantly fighting crazy wars all over the planet, but more of our attention should be on helping others, or, at a minimum, keeping them from starving. How have we gotten to this point?

We have allowed our governments to lead us down nationalistic, religious, and culturally and racially divided roads that allow the military-industrial complexes to flourish. U.S. president Dwight D. Eisenhower led one of the longest, most peaceful and prosperous periods in U.S. history. President Eisenhower brought to the presidency his prestige as commanding general of the victorious U.S. forces during WWII. He obtained a truce in Korea when he came into office, and during his two terms from 1953-1961 eased the tensions of the Cold War. One of the greatest speeches by a U.S. president, in my opinion, after Abraham Lincoln's Gettysburg Address and John Kennedy's "Ask not what your country can do for you" speech is the "Military-Industrial Complex" speech of Dwight D. Eisenhower as he left office. A few quotes of what he said in the speech are as follows: "America is today the strongest, most influential, and most productive nation in the world. Understandably proud of this preeminence, we yet realize that America's leadership and prestige depend, not merely upon our unmatched material progress, riches, and military strength, but on how we use our power in the interests of world peace and human betterment."

President Eisenhower went on to say the following, which I found to be quite profound and prescient: "In the councils of government, we must guard against the acquisition of unwarranted influence, whether sought or unsought, by the military-industrial complex. The potential for the disastrous rise of misplaced power exists and will persist." Unfortunately, I believe that this unwarranted influence has taken place. The implications of this are profound for the United States and the world.

The last part of the speech was of a caliber that all government leaders should aspire to:

We pray that peoples of all faiths, all races, all nations, may have their great human needs satisfied; that those now denied opportunity shall come to enjoy it to the full; that all who yearn for freedom may experience its spiritual blessings; that those who have freedom will understand, also, its heavy responsibilities; that all who are insensitive to the needs of others will learn charity; that the scourges of poverty, disease, and ignorance will be made to disappear from the earth, and that, in the goodness of time, all peoples will come to live together in a peace guaranteed by the binding force of mutual respect and love.

Why is it that one of America's greatest presidents of all time would warn of a potential threat from the military-industrial complex that was established to protect and defend the safety and liberty of its people? A president who had spent his life protecting and serving his country would not make his last statement in the highest position of public service flippantly. After fighting in one of the bloodiest wars in history, he, like many of us who have fought in wars, saw the absolute insanity of them. When you are involved in war and combat, you see life a lot differently. Not much rattles your cage after you have had people trying to kill you, day in and day out, for long periods of time. After you have been exposed to combat, you become mellower and more serene in normal everyday life. You appreciate every moment and the joys that living in this world can bring. If you had the influence to steer events in a direction so that war would not be waged again, you would do everything in your power, short of jeopardizing others, to stop wars.

Most conflicts could be prevented from happening to begin with. If conflicts could not be prevented, then they could most assuredly be over in one-third of the time that most of them last. The amount of time, money, materials, human lives, and suffering that is spent is far beyond what is actually required.

I have seen the waste of war for six years and in several countries. The troops are not allowed to carry the fight to its conclusion; they are restricted in rules of engagement (ROE) to the point where it's unsafe and almost insures the enemy has all the advantages. "Rules of engagement" is literally lawyer speak for the guidelines that determine when, where, how, who, and how much force you can apply to hostile threats. I remember ROEs that would change on a daily basis when I fought in the Panama invasion. I remember, too, in Mosul, Iraq, where I was lining up an advance visit by Ambassador Bremer. I was talking to the U.S. Army force on the joint Iraqi and American training base about attacks. I was shocked to hear the officer in charge tell me that the previous night they had watched a mortar team set up to fire on their compound and had to request permission to fire on the terrorists. They waited and waited for a decision and none came. Eventually, I was told, the terrorists fired on the base. "So then you fired at them?" I asked. "No," he replied, because the troops were not allowed to fire unless their lives were directly in danger. "But they had fired on the compound already, so what was the problem with trying to stop them then?" I asked. I was told that their ROEs stated that the shells had to actually land inside their compound, close to their location, before they could engage the enemy. They almost missed the opportunity to fire on the terrorists because they shot the mortars and were speeding away before the shells landed in the compound.

I was incredulous, and I thought perhaps it was an anomaly, but unfortunately it's like this everywhere wars are currently being waged. I had some of my SEAL team buddies tell me that the base that they were living on in Iraq was getting constantly mortared. They checked in with the security officer and found out that they knew the mortars were coming from a specific house and neighborhood close to the base. He asked the SEAL team if they would like to do a raid that night and see what they could come up with. My friends said that they went to the house and not only found shells and mortar tubes set up on the roof, but saw more on another roof and raided that location. While on that raid, they saw even more roofs with mortar positions and knew that a bigger operation needed to be launched. The team went back to the base security officer to report what they had found. The mortaring of the base stopped for three nights and then resumed again. The SEAL team asked if a raid had been launched and was informed that it was not approved and weren't given a reason why. To me, it seems as if the wars are being purposely manipulated for the strict reason that someone is benefiting from letting them drag on.

But who could benefit from all this conflict and fighting? Surely not the soldiers doing the fighting and dying on both sides of the conflict. Not the civilians who are caught in the cross fire. Not the infrastructure of the country that's being destroyed by the conflict. No one benefits except the companies that are in line to make a profit from these conflicts. Profit is the motive, plain and simple. I have been involved in serving my country for over thirty years now, and I have always believed that what I've trained and bled for was the right thing. I must say in all honesty that I no longer believe in this system because I can see that the corruption that Eisenhower warned us about has unfolded under our noses. I am not pointing a finger against the brave men and women who are still on the lines fighting and dying for what they believe is a worthy cause. I still work with these people and stand by them. I am speaking against the system that is using all of us for the selfish gain of a few.

In the monetary society which most of the world is currently based on, profit is the motivating factor; companies are in the business of profit and then greater profit on top of that, ad infinitum. That is the way a capitalist system works.

In 1965, CEOs in major companies made twenty-four times more than the average worker. In 1980, CEOs made forty times more than the average worker. In 2007, the average CEO from a Fortune

500 company made three hundred sixty-four times more than an average worker and over seventy times the pay of a four-star U.S. Army general. According to IRS figures, the richest one percent of Americans reported 22 percent of the nation's total adjusted gross income in 2006. Need I go on?

The military-industrial complex is going to do whatever it takes to stay profitable and to preserve itself. If a weapons system is going to be discontinued, then the company is going to look for a way to make other weapon systems that they can continue to profit from. The only way this system is going to stop perpetuating itself is if the entire monetary structure throughout the world changes.

The State Department reported there were more than twenty-two thousand deaths from terrorism in 2007. That's sixty people per day. By contrast, 9,125,000 people die every year from starvation, or twenty-five thousand a day. The UN's World Food Programme (WFP) said that with voluntary contributions from the world's wealthy nations, the WFP feeds seventy-three million people in seventy-eight countries, less than one-tenth of the total number of the world's undernourished. Its agreed budget for 2008 was $2.9 billion. The budget for the U.S. military in 2008 was $1.473 trillion.

We are focusing our resources on problems that are for the most part out of proportion to what we are being led to believe. Hunger is just one example of many scourges that could be easily eliminated forever from the earth if resources weren't wasted on outdated weaponry. Is terrorism a problem? Absolutely. But the amount of energy that is being put into this problem is way out of proportion. We have the capacity on our planet to provide water, food, housing, hospitals, and education to everyone in the world, but it is not going to happen as long as profit is a deciding factor.

In *Political Observations, 1795,* James Madison said, "Of all the enemies to public liberty, war is, perhaps, the most to be dreaded because it comprises and develops the germ of every other. War is the parent of armies; from these proceed debts and taxes... known instruments for bringing the many under the domination of the few... No nation could preserve its freedom in the midst of continual warfare." I'm not advocating a communist system, or any system of government currently in operation for that matter. We all know that they are for the most part in collusion with and motivated by the same corrupting monetary system. What I'm advocating is a completely new system of exchange that is intuitively based on what humanity decides is best. An intuitively based system would not benefit the few while others are suffering. It would not force others to do the bidding of a few groups that control most of the power and will stop at nothing to maintain it. An intuitively based world that is awakening to the corruption that now permeates systems that our society has trusted for generations will not allow these systems to continue. Intuitively informed individuals will know that for any system to function, it needs the cooperation of the masses. Intuitively based leadership would not allow a corrupt monetary system like the one we currently have in place to continue. For an intuitive based leadership to exist, it must have the backing of an intuitive society, because the two are mutually supportive of each other. As a collective, the further we advance intuitively, the faster corrupt systems will deteriorate and crumble as they have already begun to do.

"THE DOCTOR OF THE FUTURE WILL GIVE NO MEDICINE, BUT WILL INTEREST HIS PATIENTS IN THE CARE OF THE HUMAN FRAME; IN DIET AND IN THE CAUSE AND PREVENTION OF DISEASE."

◊ *Thomas Edison* ◊

Chapter 19

KINESIOLOGY

Kinesiology is the science that focuses on how the body functions and moves. As a SEAL, a high level of physical fitness is paramount to job performance. Understanding the human body's physical movement and how to maximize fitness training is always a focus for those in a line of work that demands it. During the first phase of our basic SEAL training, I would learn techniques that I would master after many years as a SEAL and later as an instructor. I would lead the toughest physical training (PT) evolutions at BUD/S, where I remember at one time doing sets of pull-ups to 180 reps, sets of dips between bars to 450 reps total, sets of pushups to 450 reps total, and—the real clincher—the nonstop cross-arm sit-ups of 1000, plus the class number. The highest number of cross-arm sit-ups I remember doing was 1189, and it took thirty minutes alone to complete. In one class, while I was leading this three-hour marathon PT, three guys quit during this evolution, which was rare because PTs were usually a break for the class compared to other evolutions. On this particular day, though, the instructor staff was in rare form and was making sure all the students performed all the repetitions. I would go into a zone, or detached meditation, while doing these high repetitions and would see the instructors, out of my peripheral vision, moving around, giving extra incentive to those who were not keeping up. Through the loud, anguished groans and whining, I could hear the instructors yelling at students who hadn't learned the inner discipline to put out yet. In between my cadence calls, I would call out to the students to push through the pain. Once you have pushed through the pain zone, which your ego keeps resisting because it always wants to be comfortable, you can accomplish amazing levels of performance. So in between the screaming of the students and the shouts of the instructors would come my monotone "push through the pain" call to the students, and if they could see through their pain, they would see me as an example in front of them and join me in my own pain-induced nirvana. Learning to push through the ego's mind tricks was a prerogative to success as a SEAL, and for these tadpoles to become frogmen, they would have to learn to slip into this state of mind quietly and in an instant.

Some of my favorite lines were "If you think this is tough, you're wrong, because this is the basics, hence the name Basic Underwater Demolition SEAL training" and "I have been far more miserable, cold, tired, etc., than you are right now." Several of the other instructors would pipe in with an "Amen to that," which was true in that we had all experienced far more discomfort in the Teams that we had to push through than these students were ever going to experience in BUD/S. In the beginning of training, that psychological ploy was effective to get a few weak links to call it quits, but after a while you couldn't get them to go no matter what you threw at them, which of course is what we desired, so then, once they had gained our fickle respect, we would move on to imparting other knowledge.

I would push my own knowledge of the development of the human body through reading the works of Steve Reeves, Joe Weider, and Arnold Schwarzenegger, seven-time Mr. Olympia winner, and many others who would inspire me to compete and win many trophies in natural bodybuilding contests while still a Navy SEAL.

After I started the hand-to-hand course for the SEAL teams, I took my knowledge of kinesiology to another level by studying and applying what I was learning through martial fighting to a broader awareness of capabilities within the human body.

A martial arts teacher once showed me how to influence the body's energy field by running his hands along my sides and then pressing down on my outstretched arms, which then collapsed as if I had no energy to hold them up. This opened a door into the unseen world of energy that I have thoroughly investigated to come up with astonishing results. I have gone deeply into this world of unseen energy after that time, when I was shown but not taught what I had experienced. I would have to find out this information on my own, which is a crafty but frustrating thing that masters like to do with initiates. This is a hidden door of mysteries that few will discover, fewer open, and fewer still can venture into. We all have access to this door, but you have to be a searcher and not expect someone to bring it to you and drop it in your lap. There are many self- serving groups that have no interest in your finding the secrets of life because you cannot serve them if you have your own power and wisdom.

A master in a sermon once said: "Ask, and it will be given to you; seek, and you will find; knock, and it will be opened to you. For everyone who asks receives, and he who seeks finds, and to him who knocks it will be opened." Wisdom can be gained from those who have knowledge, experience, and intuitive understanding. Acquiring your own wisdom is an essential key to living a good life.

I am going to open a door for everyone that is reading this right now. I am going to cast some of my pearls out, although I know some will trample upon them, but others will invariably take these pearls for themselves and wisely use them at their discretion.

The door that I speak of is called applied kinesiology, and this is the wisdom that was used to influence my energy field by the martial arts master that I spoke about earlier. One of the greatest teachers of this knowledge is Dr. David R. Hawkins. His book *Power vs. Force: The Hidden Determinants of Human Behavior* is a landmark work in this field and one that is fascinating and compelling in that it requires you to learn from the external to the internal, something most Western thinkers find difficult or even impossible.

There are occasions where East meets West and the two combine to synergistically create a wisdom that transcends and can inspire both cultures, and applied kinesiology is one of these wisdoms.

I will begin to open the door for you by giving you an example that I teach people. This example can be tried by anyone as long as you have someone else to work with. I usually show the technique and then I discuss the effects.

I will have someone hold their arms straight out at their sides with palms down. I will then press down on their arms while they resist me and test their muscle strength. I will usually press down with a good amount of energy so that they can feel the resistance in their muscles. I will then have them drop their arms, after which I will run my hands down close along their bodies, starting at the top and working my way down to the ground. I will then have them raise their arms again and press down on their arms after they have extended them, and they will invariably collapse with very little effort on my part.

What does this demonstrate? It demonstrates that the body has unseen energy fields that are naturally strong and balanced, when not disturbed. When I sweep the body with my hands, however, I push the energetic fields of the body downwards and cause them to move downward so that when I push down on the outstretched arms again, it is easy to push them down because that is the direction in which your energy fields are moving now. If I were to reverse the process, by sweeping upwards along the body, it would rebalance the fields and even make you slightly stronger.

This is usually a real eye opener for anyone who has not witnessed this phenomenon before, whether they are Western or Eastern. How does this connect East and West? Eastern thought is inner-world dependant, and the energy fields are part of our inner, unseen world, so it is easy for right hemisphere-dominant people to grasp this concept. Western thought is outer-world dependent and mainly left hemisphere-dominant, so people who need to see the outer physical effects of this exercise can visibly see and grasp this concept as well. Because both hemispheres of the brain are stimulated in this exercise, it is an excellent way to start people on the road to understanding a larger part of themselves that they may not have connected with before.

I have encountered a few skeptics over the years to this technique, and my wife, who witnessed me teach and demonstrate this technique to hundreds of people, was one of the biggest skeptics for a long time. While she was convinced when she first saw me teach this technique and perform it on her, she later saw someone supposedly debunk this technique on television. It took nearly two years for her to finally get it again, and most of that time was spent quietly watching me refine my teaching skills and expand upon what I was already teaching in regards to applied kinesiology. When my wife decides to become hardheaded no matter how much proof or rational logic I present her with, I usually back off and let her learn at her own pace, often the hard way. It's funny that now when she argues a point and I get quiet and say "Okay, we'll see," she knows something is up and she may have rushed to judgment, and she quickly reassesses with a more open mind. Many skeptics will argue that I influence the outcome by suggestion, but I will perform several different double-blind techniques to prove otherwise. Another argument is that I or others influence the outcome by our personal influence, but that is my whole point for this demonstration to begin with. We are influencing our world constantly with our thoughts and actions, and that is what the tool of applied kinesiology shows us.

Masaru Emoto represents a very good example of projecting your thoughts and being able to see a physical manifestation in the book *The Hidden Messages in Water*. Using high-speed photography, Dr. Emoto discovered that crystals formed in frozen water reveal changes when specific thoughts are directed toward them. If negative thoughts are directed at them, they form grotesque distorted shapes. But if positive thoughts are directed at the crystals as they form, then beautifully shaped crystals in intricate patterns show up under a microscope. You can also see an example of this in the movie *What the Bleep Do We Know!?*

Once I understood the power of our thoughts, the science of quantum physics that explains this power to influence our world, and the powerful experience I had with sending out love to counter an attack on our convoy, I eventually advanced this love-energy-thought-knowledge to the point where I send it out into the environment to actually stop attacks that I intuit are about to happen. I haven't been in an area since I began doing this that has been attacked, even though we know we have specific threats against our group, and I have intuited that these attacks are coming. Imagine if more of us started doing this. Peace on Earth is within our grasp, and the science of intuition will speed its arrival.

As a collective, humanity is moving from base physical awareness to an expanded intellect, and in the near future will evolve rapidly into an intuitional being. The time has come for us to not look at our past to describe who we are, but to look at our now moment to describe our future. We are moving so rapidly away from old hierarchical systems that forced us into a way of seeing ourselves that the past no longer shapes our amazing intellect and expanding consciousness any longer. Hierarchical based political, economic, religious, and educational systems around the world are crumbling, because they no longer support this rapid evolvement of the intuition.

This evolving process has been accelerating the closer we get to the October 2012 time frame when the Mayan calendars all come to an end. The Peruvians say that we will evolve from Homo sapiens into Homo spiritus, and the Hopi have said that we are entering the fifth world, which will be a golden age. This new age will not come without growing pains, but as the old systems collapse, as they will and must, they will be rebuilt with the guidance of the intuitive awakening that is touching all of humanity. North and South American indigenous tribes are based in Eastern mystical thought and are a bridge living in the Western analytical thought world; this interaction will help usher in the new intuitional world, or golden age. The division between East and West thought has been the one of the biggest hindrances to our advancement into Homo spiritus, and that gulf has been rapidly closing. We are in one of the most exciting times in our evolution as a species. Now is not a time for fear of the unknown, but a time to allow ourselves to be open to the new changes and know that they are happening for our greatest good.

"THOUGH SYNCHRONISTIC PHENOMENA OCCUR IN TIME AND SPACE, THEY MANIFEST A REMARKABLE INDEPENDENCE OF BOTH OF THESE INDISPENSABLE DETERMINANTS OF PHYSICAL EXISTENCE AND HENCE DO NOT CONFORM TO THE LAW OF CAUSALITY."

◊ *Carl Jung* ◊

Mysterium Coniunctionis

Chapter 20

SYNCHRONICITY

Within a few minutes of touching down in Baghdad on my first contracting trip, Saddam Hussein was captured. While this may seem like a simple coincidence to some, to me it was not. I had been in a sacred sweat lodge with a Native American friend several weeks prior, and we had prayed with the group within the sweat lodge that Saddam would be captured. We had felt at the time that this would help secure victory and would make Iraq and the world a safer place. Afterward, we had joked that it would be funny if they captured him the moment I arrived in the country. In a synchronistic twist, it did happen that way a few weeks later when the plane I arrived on touched down as Saddam Hussein was simultaneously being pulled out of a hole in the ground. That same night, I found out that Saddam was captured after we took Ambassador Bremer to see him as he was getting a medical inspection. I smiled to myself that night because I had come to realize that coincidences are rarely that, but rather coordinated events in your life that you consciously or unconsciously attract and manifest by the power of your thoughts.

Swiss psychologist Carl Jung coined the term synchronicity and believed that many experiences perceived as coincidence were not merely due to chance but instead suggested the manifestation of parallel events or circumstances reflecting this governing dynamic.

Of course, there are other factors involved, and if we study quantum physics, we begin to realize that there is a scientific awareness that explains how the universe around us works, and by becoming aware of it and working within that paradigm, we can literally change the world around us with our thoughts. We are coming into the understanding of some of the mysteries of life and the realization that they can actually be solved; old, outdated ways of thinking can be changed into a greater understanding of our world and how we interact within it.

The ancient Greeks, Socrates, Plato, and Aristotle, were answering some of these questions as many as 2500 years ago, and presenting the case for understanding and accepting concepts outside of our physical understanding through metaphysics. During the same time frame, Democritus and Leucippus were even describing atoms long before we had any visual proof of their existence.

So we should not always necessarily have to have physical, tangible proof to recognize that certain events affect our physical three-dimensional reality before we accept the possibility of their influence. Nor should we completely discount events that fall outside of our recognized and accepted reality. To do so would be limiting and debilitating to the progression of humanity and the higher self.

Synchronistic events can be seen in nature by the coordinated movement of flocks of birds or schools of fish. Physicists call this type of coordinated movement "entrainment" or the law of conservation. I have worked with teams that operate very close to or at this level, and it is extremely rewarding because you can accomplish teamwork at an impossible level of accepted reality. Some of the most visible human aspects of entrainment can be witnessed through military groups like the U.S. Marine Corps silent drill team or the Navy's Blue Angels flight demonstration team. Teams like this are aligned toward a common goal, and there is a high level of cooperation, harmony, and entrainment.

Synchronistic events help explain synchronicity by their ability to accomplish seemingly impossible physical realities. By repeatedly practicing together, groups reach a point where they are able to reach a higher level of reality than what is normally thought to be physically possible. When synchronistic events are combined with an awareness of the possibility of things happening outside the realm of our current knowledge base, we begin to open up to things that we previously did not perceive or thought impossible and therefore discounted as flukes of nature.

The Law of Attraction also helps to answer how synchronistic events unfold. The Law of Attraction, like the Law of Gravity, has specific principles that, when applied, cause these laws to appear or work in our conscious surroundings. Of course when ancient man dropped something from his hand and it fell to the ground, he did not think to himself *Ah, the law of gravity at work*. He just knew that dropping the rock caused it to fall. When a spear was thrown, or a bow and arrow was used, he knew through cause and effect, observation, and consistent principles of action, that the spear or arrow would go so far before it came back to earth. Later, when Sir Isaac Newton coined the term gravity and it became adopted as a scientific law, it opened the door to further understanding and the advancement of human consciousness to a different level.

Unfortunately, as is often the case, information that is outside the narrow confines of current accepted dogma can run into trouble with whatever group is in control or has power to control information. In 1633, the astronomer Galileo was tried as a heretic and forced to recant his theory that the Earth revolved around the sun. Church teaching at the time placed Earth at the center of the universe. It was not until nearly four hundred years later, in 1992, that Pope John Paul II declared that the ruling against Galileo was an error resulting from "tragic mutual incomprehension."

While I think it highly unlikely that I'll be forced to recant (or worse, be burned at the stake for espousing) some of the controversial information outlined in this book, I do believe that we are being restricted from reaching our full potential as spiritual beings having a human being experience.

Comments like the following from the Rev. José Gabriel Funes, the Jesuit director of the Vatican Observatory, who said that "the vastness of the universe means it is possible there could be other forms of life outside Earth, even intelligent ones" leads me to believe that we could be turning a corner in accepting that there is much more than the limited world we see. Funes went on to say that the universe potentially holds many of God's children and that we are all brothers and sisters: "Just as we consider earthly creatures as 'a brother,' and 'sister,' why should we not talk about an 'extraterrestrial brother'? It would still be part of creation." Funes, speaking for the Vatican, really helped turn a corner and bridge a gap by saying that science, especially astronomy, "doesn't contradict our faith" because aliens would still be God's creatures. Ruling out the existence of aliens, he said, would be like "putting limits" on God's creative freedom.

I wonder how the Vatican would feel about my idea that we are all capable of telepathy and practice it, often unknowingly, many times throughout the day. Synchronistic events happen and we think they are just coincidences, but we are attracting them to us by our thoughts and through telepathy. Embracing this idea as a possibility opens up a whole universe of exciting human potential, as I will explain in the next chapter.

Whenever I desire something to materialize in my life, I have learned to focus on the desired outcome as if it is already in my life. I dreamed for years of becoming a Navy SEAL, and when events started to unfold that opened doors for its materialization in my life, I was thrilled. I didn't know about the law of attraction then, but when I look back, I can see the effects of what transpired in my life over time by what I most focused on.

I have learned that synchronicity works outside our current

three-dimensional laws and our understanding of those laws. If you are tied to those laws, then you are like a ship without a rudder, being cast to and fro at the whim of the ocean currents. Synchronistic events that occur seemingly at random in your life are signposts guiding you to what you are searching for in life. If you notice them for what they are and recognize that they are leading you, like a door that opens as you approach it, they will bring you one step closer to the fulfillment of your desires.

I remember when I wanted to start competing in bodybuilding contests. It was a dream that I'd had for many years. The timing was right in my life, so I began to focus my energy in that direction. I had no idea what to do other than read bodybuilding magazines every month, but they weren't really giving me the information I needed. I wanted to take it one step further, so I was open to something but had no idea how to proceed. I was living near the beach in a condominium at the time, and the Navy pilot couple that owned the condo across from me was transferred to another state, and a bodybuilding couple moved in to rent their condominium. I noticed this for what it was, a door opening to what I desired most at the time. I eventually became good friends with the couple, and I was shown how to diet properly, which up to then I didn't realize was important. I began to develop the physique necessary to compete and then started preparing a posing routine with the help and direction of my new friends. I even met and became friends with some of the guys who were going to compete in the same natural bodybuilding competition that I was, which was being held in my gym. They gave me even more direction as to what to expect and do to prepare for the competition, as they had done the same one the year before. I had worked out at this gym for two years and had never even noticed these guys before. The competition came, and I won my first ever trophy! What a blast it was and an amazing fulfillment of a dream. I've gone on to compete in several contests since that time and will forever remember how synchronistic events led me to the fulfillment of a lifelong dream.

If you want to fulfill a dream or manifest anything in your life, then you have to focus on the positive outcome of your desires or they will not manifest themselves. Your desire has to be unwavering and focused.

As I write this book, I have no idea how to get it published or the process I will need to go through to do it. My desire is to share the knowledge that I have with as many people who are open to it as possible. Like a team player who knows he has information that will benefit the team if shared, I am doing my best to help out. I have the confidence of past success and the example of others to help me stay focused on my dream and to trust that synchronistic events will unfold to guide me to its fulfillment. If you are reading this book, then you know that I trusted that synchronistic events would occur to guide me to the fulfillment of my desires and that those events did transpire as I desired them to.

Because synchronistic events line up outside our three-dimensional worldview, many people are quick to discount them as a mere coincidence and dismiss them. To dismiss them would be the equivalent of slamming a door that has just magically opened in front of you, or to take the rudder off your ship and just drift, hoping that the tides will carry you to your desires.

The higher self works only from the heart, and if we connect with our hearts and learn how to manifest from our hearts, instead of our heads, then we will manifest and connect with synchronistic events more easily. Manifesting from our heads or right brain creates an egoistic world of dualism: a world where our thoughts create a space for negative events and darkness. Manifesting from the heart and right brain is the way earth-based indigenous tribes have created their reality for millennia. The non-earth-based cultures have been manifesting from the left brain and creating chaos and destruction. The two different cultures need each other to progress into the higher dimensional energies now entering the earth. As the earth moves closer to the galactic center where the energies for transformation come from, then we will see these shifts transpiring. Anyone who has worked in a hospital or on a police force can tell you what happens during full moons. Violence escalates among those who are unbalanced or lean toward negativity. The energies which are already entering our world as we transition from our twelve thousand year descent into darkness, away from the light of the galactic center, and move back into a twelve thousand year ascent into the light. We will be transformed as has happened several times in earth's history. Many ancient indigenous cultures have left us information that supports this change, such as the Hopi and Mayan prophecies. From a scientific standpoint, these changes are already manifesting in our galaxy.

Habibullo Abdussamatov, head of space research at St. Petersburg's Pulkovo Astronomical Observatory in Russia, says there is evidence that the current global warming on Earth is being caused by changes in the sun.

Evidence of a pole shift on Jupiter's moon Europa and polar wander on Earth and Mars indicate that the galactic center's energies are impacting our sun, which in turn is affecting the planets and planetary satellites in our entire galaxy.

NASA evidence points to the following:

Ice caps on Mars melted fifty percent in one year. Saturn's magnetic fields are increasing. Earths ice caps have thinned forty percent in the past decade. Our sun's magnetic field has increased 230 percent in the past century.

As Earth moves closer to the galactic center, we will all see a great shift in consciousness. Focusing on the energy of the heart has brought about a rapid shift in my awareness and my intuition. The more I have learned to focus on the heart, its connection to the right brain, and then the pineal gland and the higher self, the faster I have begun to manifest my dreams and desires.

Follow your hearts' desires and move your consciousness to a place centered in love, and you will begin seeing wonderful synchronicities begin to manifest in your life, which are your signposts that you are on the right track. As the energies from the galactic core increasingly manifest on earth you will begin to witness the level of manifesting change increase on Earth. You are probably already noticing how quickly the economy's old negative energy is crumbling. This will quickly be replaced by a new manifested energy that is positive and matches the energy from the galactic core. Continue to observe this increasing anomaly throughout all aspects of our society until it is no longer foreign to you. Do not fear these changes as they are for the better as they will replace the energies of fear with those of love. You can then begin to focus your thoughts more on what your hearts desires are and experience their increased manifestation.

"THE MIND DOES NOTHING BUT TALK, AND ASK QUESTIONS, AND SEARCH FOR MEANINGS. THE HEART DOES NOT TALK, DOES NOT ASK QUESTIONS, DOES NOT SEARCH FOR MEANINGS. IT SILENTLY MOVES TOWARD GOD AND SURRENDERS ITSELF TO HIM."

◊ *Francis of Assisi* ◊

Chapter 21

A WORLD AWAKENING

On my first trip to Baghdad, Iraq, I had an incredible experience one night that continues to shape and inspire me to this day. Every night for several weeks after Saddam Hussein had been captured, the area of the palace grounds had been mortared, usually around midnight to just before dawn. At first it was unnerving, but as the fire was almost always ineffective, we learned, after initially being jarred awake by the explosions, to listen for whether it was close, and, if not a danger, then we would drift back asleep.

Inside the walled palace grounds was where most of the state department personnel, contractors, and military slept, either in tents or thin metal trailers that would offer no protection against a well-placed mortar shell. When Saddam had been captured and the news released to the public, the local Iraqis took to the streets and celebrated by firing pistols and AK-47 assault rifles into the air. Shooting guns in the air is a common practice in the Middle East that usually occurs after Friday weddings and is an accepted and traditional way of rejoicing. Saddam's capture caused a full day and night of celebratory fire and was unnerving at first because we thought gun battles were occurring all around us and we were sure to be soon overwhelmed as there were so many. When we learned it was the locals having a good time after learning of Saddam's capture, we breathed a sigh of relief, but that was soon replaced with the thought of what was happening with all those rounds that were going up in the air and must eventually fall back down to earth? My roommate and I soon found out when we returned to our trailer for the night as the sound of gunfire continued all around us outside the walls of the palace complex. Lying on my roommate's pillow was a bullet that had penetrated the thin metal roof and come to rest right where his head would have lain. Needless to say, that was a restless night of sleep.

Miraculously, no one had been injured in the nightly mortar attacks over the past several weeks. One night during this time, I had what is called an out of body experience (OBE). During an OBE, you are completely awake and aware, but your awareness is outside of your body. OBEs should not be confused with lucid dreaming, where you are in a dream, or not in our three dimensional world, but are very aware and it seems like you are awake. In a lucid dream, you are aware and *in* your body, while in an OBE, you are aware and *out* of your body.

I had never experienced an OBE before, but had wondered what they were like. During my experience, I remember the feeling of floating and being aware that I was above my body, and a thrill went through me as I realized what was happening. I remember reading how people would look down at their bodies and see them lying asleep. I now looked down to see if I could view my body, and to my horror realized that the trailer was destroyed and what looked like bricks were strewn all around. I had never seen any bricks around our trailer before, so this confused me. I looked closer still in the darkness to see if I could find my body and saw that it was mangled and torn. The thought went through me that I was seeing my dead body and that my spirit had departed it and I was now looking down on my body for the last time. I had the thought that I was sad that I would never see my children again, or my wife, and the last thought I remember thinking was that I felt I was finally figuring out life and I wanted to pass my knowledge on and be able to help people.

I then had the feeling of a presence and looked upward to see the face of an angel with huge wings outspread, hovering just above the scene of destruction below. The look on the face of this angel was one of complete love of an intensity that is indescribable. As we both hovered, gazing at each other, a complete peace washed over my being, and then I saw a brilliant flash of orange light, and I awoke with a start in my bed inside the trailer. I immediately shouted excitedly at my sleeping roommate to ask if he had seen the flash of light just as a thunderous explosion went off. He stirred and mumbled incoherently, and I realized how foolish my question was as we lived in a trailer with no windows. I lay back down and began to marvel at what had just occurred. I was happy to be alive and in my body, and I wondered about the experience I'd just witnessed and what it represented before drifting off to a deep sleep.

My life was hectic, and for the next several days I had little time to reflect on what had occurred on the night of my OBE. Several days later, I had a few moments of free time, and I decided I would try and track down where the bricks in my dream may have come from. I went to our berthing area to look at the wall that was behind our trailer, and as I rounded the corner to head toward our block, I noticed that the wall was broken and torn in an area I hadn't noticed before. I looked in stunned amazement at the wall and realized it was a brick wall that was covered by a layer of mortar and thus resembling solid concrete. I would learn over the next several years while traveling around the Middle East that this is the way they build walls around homes and in the homes themselves. All walls, external and internal, are made of brick covered with a layer of mortar. This is one of the reasons earthquakes are so devastating and result in such a great loss of life in this area of the world. The walls collapse easily because they are just a thin layer of brick and mortar that is largely unsupported and reinforced. What I had thought was a large cement wall behind our trailer was nothing more than a bunch of bricks that would easily have collapsed in an explosion. I also learned that the explosion that had happened the night I'd had the OBE was a rocket attack—the first of many deadly rocket attacks to come. That explained the orange flash I had seen, because mortars aren't propelled by a rocket. I had also thought the explosion was unusually loud but thought maybe I had been half in and half outside the trailer. Now I realized that it was the flash from a rocket that had been fired, and the rocket used carries a larger warhead than the mortar rounds that had been used. The rockets that were now being used were very accurate, and over the coming months would be used to inflict many casualties and close calls on the surrounding palace complex and green zone. This helped reinforce the belief that I'd had an OBE.

The night after my OBE, a military AC-130H Spectre gunship began circling at night overhead and hammered insurgent targets outside the green zone for hours every night for several weeks. I had worked with these aircraft many times as a Navy SEAL during training missions and several times during the Panama Invasion. The targeting equipment and firepower is amazing. Once, during a mission to track down General Noriega, we were in position outside a house that he was possibly hiding in when we heard a noise on the other side of a wall. Our communications guy radioed to a circling Spectre to find out if they could identify what was on the other side of the wall. They radioed back that it was only a dog and they had been tracking it for a while. What a great asset to have on your side, and that was the technology of the late 1980s! Now, fifteen years later, this aircraft had been updated several times with far more advanced technology. The firepower is just as impressive, as it uses high-tech targeting systems to put 7.62 mm miniguns, 20 mm Gatling guns, 40 mm cannon, and 105 howitzer shells wherever they need to go. We were all happy to hear Spectre circling overhead the night after the rocket attack, but it was a little unnerving that there were so many targets for them to shoot at throughout the night. This was long overdue, and with the arrival of this impressive aircraft, we were able to sleep soundly again throughout the night without any mortar or rocket attacks for several weeks.

I started researching angels and archangels a couple of days after my OBE to see if I could find which one I had seen that night. Although I had attended church on occasion as a child and young man, I was never a big church follower, but would call myself deeply spiritual if asked about my spiritual persuasion. I did not have a large background and knowledge of the different angels and archangels, but I have always believed in their existence. As virtually all major religions have links to the same angels and archangels, it was easy to do research and find pictures and descriptions. I would eventually find what I was searching for as I came across beautiful pictures of Archangel Michael that left no doubt in my mind that this was the archangel's face I had gazed upon and the eyes that had pierced into mine and touched my soul on a very deep level. The love that emanated from Archangel Michael's eyes even in pictures profoundly moved me and reconnected me with that moment during my OBE. The love that pored from his eyes into mine would transform me over time and be used by me over the next several years as I traveled the world's war torn hot spots, protecting others and keeping them from danger. I would learn from reading of this powerful archangel that he is a protector of those in danger, and I have no doubt that he had shielded me that night from an event that was about to happen in our three-dimensional time. I saw a future event of death and destruction that night before it happened and would, after that moment, be given the gift of preventing these events in the areas I would travel to by seeing them in the future and helping the groups I was with to avoid them.

I would also eventually read a book named *Home with God*, by Neale Donald Walsh of the *Conversations with God* series, about how we are often given the choice during our lives to either continue or choose to leave our bodies. This can happen for many different reasons, including getting off track from your life purpose to the point where you no longer are learning what you intended to learn before you incarnated. Often, near death experiences and being given the choice to continue will have the effect needed to get you back on track or get you moving in the direction you intended before incarnating into this life. A really good quote from Walsh's book fits perfectly with many of the themes I've covered in this book: "You experience a three-dimensional world, but you do not live in one. Ultimate Reality is far more complex than you may ever have imagined."

To be given the opportunity to continue with this life was a phenomenal gift, which would enable me to see future events and help protect people. I believe we all have inherent abilities that we have developed over our lifetimes. Some of these abilities within us are dormant because we are developing different aspects and don't need them. Some abilities don't activate until we have reached a level of development that will support the understanding and use of these abilities, and until we reach that level they will not come forward into our awareness. I have become aware that I have developed the abilities that I now use. The skills I now have did not come easy, so I don't take them for granted. A desire and a willingness to use the skills can be the only deciding factor in whether we become intuitive and learn how to access these gifts from our higher selves at all.

We are all connected and experiencing life in our own individuated experiences, but we are still ultimately as one. Every major spiritual leader that has come into this earthly plane to inform and guide us has said that we are one with the Creator and interconnected with all life. What any two people see outside of themselves will differ, but if those same two people look within the other person, they will see themselves.

Everyone is gifted in one way or another. My truths and path may not necessarily be the same as yours, but they ultimately lead to the same source and therefore the oneness we all share, for in truth there is only Oneness/Source/God or whatever you connect with as the ultimate. All of our collective gifts reverberate into our environment and ultimately impact each other like concentric waves in a pond that emanate from different locations, but, when they meet, conjoin and radiate from that point on as one. We are all like drops of water that ultimately form the ocean. Although we are as one and form a whole, we see ourselves as individual and separate, but this is an untruth. The gift of intuition is available to everyone, but to harness this gift takes patience, discipline, and desire. Once you have the gift, you can lose it if you do not continue to honor its promptings. If you do lose it or do not yet have it in your awareness, it will return whenever you are ready and willing.

Intuition is an incredible gift that all humanity can share in, and it can advance any and all areas of your life. Like a butterfly in the wind, it can flutter away as fast as you can chase it; but if you are still and silent, it will land on your outstretched hand and spread its wings so that you can marvel at its beauty and delicateness. We can be like the butterfly that was once a lowly worm and metamorphose into our intuitional selves if we can learn to believe and desire a higher level of achievement throughout every aspect of our beings. Intuition can and will be yours simply for the asking.

EPILOGUE

I hope the words in this book have provided you with inspiration and hope for an awakening intuition within yourself, an awakening to the realization that you are a powerful being and that what you do in life matters to everyone and everything else in this our world. Also know that the realization of the power of intuition is happening throughout humanity in a wave that will eventually envelop all. At times, it may not seem like an awakening is happening, as all that we seem to hear or see is how everything is far from perfect. Change is often resisted even if it is for the better, as even those who see that change could better their station in life resist for either selfish reasons or because of fear of the unknown. As we have seen in the preceding chapters of this book, fear has no place in an awakened humanity and therefore will eventually be replaced by the strongest force in the universe: love.

Shortly after the tragic incidents of 9/11, a unique experience began to happen to me. I was working at the Naval Academy at the time and often wore my dress uniform with all my ribbons and SEAL insignia and was often stopped by people in the community and thanked for my service. This was the first time in over twenty-two years of service to the United States that anyone had ever done this to me. While I had always seen myself, the people that I worked with in the military and other agencies that were focused on our national defense as unsung heroes, it was still quite rewarding to be thanked. My intent as I wrote this book, at the urging of several friends and family, was to impart what I have learned through selfless sacrifice to my country and often the world as a whole. My service continues but in a different format now.

The words in this book come from my heart to your heart. Know that the things that I have done, you can do and far greater.

THE INTUITIVE WARRIOR

Resurrection

The beauty of writing a 2nd edition book many years after the release of a new book is that you experience the thrill of discovering what impact the original had on the world.

I felt that *The Intuitive Warrior* would be an idea ahead of its time and that the experiences and ideas that I seeded into the collective consciousness would take time to germinate.

The type of person that I thought would be impacted the most would be military warriors like myself and those of like mind. Police, firemen, martial artists and those that aspired to manifest these noble ways of developing themselves and using those skills in the service of humanity. This group of focused individuals and team players would be the people attracted to the cover and would peek inside to see if there was something that would inform and motivate them, I believed.

I was right in a sense but in totality not by a long shot. Women are the ones that are most attracted to this work and in retrospect it's obvious why. Ladies are often more intuitive as the intuitive realm is feminine by nature. Females of all ages are natural team builders through playing with dolls, birthing, raising and keeping families together. As a little boy I often had best friends that were girls. This was unwittingly preparing the intuitive mind early on.

Team building skills came on a much deeper level through my active participation in sports and in the SEAL Teams. This constant exposure built a deep understanding of the value of being a team player which requires intuitive skills on reading others and instantly reacting at the perfect time for maximum effect. I also instructed many others on becoming exceptional team players. Being a master training specialist required extraordinary creativity and observational skills which women are also often masters at.

As you can imagine my masculine analytical and physical side was very developed as an athlete and SEAL. Over my 35 years in the

SEAL Teams and the CIA, often in combat zones, I naturally began to develop the softer side and bring in the intuitive skills that would take me from a great warrior to an exceptional warrior.

My observations of teammates over the course of my entire life led me to realize that everyone that reached a master level was tapping into their intuitive skills. I would often notice that the high performing women I worked with in the CIA were impeccably balanced in both the masculine and feminine side. The ones that did not become high achievers often had become unbalanced while trying to compete in a masculine dominated culture.

I would often help guide these women in reconnecting with their intuitive side as I did when working with the woman that helped find the worlds most wanted terrorist, Osama ben Laden.

Over the last 12 years since the release of *The Intuitive Warrior* I learned to apply my intuitive skills in many diverse areas of life. Becoming a savvy investor knowing when and what to invest in. Taking the entrepreneurial spirit, seeming to mysteriously blossom forth since I was a little boy when I sold lemonade from my red wagon, and applying intuition to it, I built upon several successful business models developed from scratch. I went from speaking to large audiences in the military and civilian realm with power point presentations to speaking with no presentation material or notes, speaking from the intuitive heart for several series of lectures effortlessly. These intuitively guided, speaking from the heart events are as you can probably imagine much better received than the well managed analytical events.

Over the period of several decades, I also engaged in instructing professionals across a broad spectrum of fields of endeavor including brain and heart surgeons, musicians, actors, opera singers, politicians, SWAT Teams, firefighters, martial artists and many more that became better in their fields after learning to unleash their own intuition.

Other amazing revelations I've had over time relate to the Arch Angel Michael experience I share in the latter half of this book. Just that experience alone has constantly informed me over the years.

Initially after that supernatural encounter I doubted it was real. Over time, I learned that not only was that a life altering event frozen in the memory of my minds eye for all time, but also a download of special abilities. Not completely believing I'd witnessed a real Arch Angel initially changed to a knowing over the next days, months and years. Doubting as I've come to learn is an inhibitor to achievement in life. Once the disbelief was replaced with knowing I really started shifting my psychic abilities into ultra-high gear.

I started to have remote viewing skills advance from real time to days out seeing terrorist attacks coming in Iraq in early 2003 before any attacks had happened. Then the ability increased to a week out and the accuracy was within a few minutes in time. I saw details that had never come through before. Then the abilities increased to remote influencing. Again, just affecting things real time then eventually to the point where some of the things I've influenced have lasted for years.

I've also had my intuitive skills spontaneously expand as I began to pick up on earthquakes and storms. Then they expanded again to the point where I have influenced these earth events with consciousness. Within the SEAL Teams we learned to teach each other the skills we mastered and that is exactly what my intention has become with this work. While in combat zones in the Middle East I began to teach others how to recognize and develop these natural skills we all inherently possess. The only challenge to unleashing intuitive skills are believing that you can, don't doubt and practice.

I remember as a young man just turning 21 years old on the day Hell Week training started that I had great difficulty with the cold water. The instructor staff have an intuitive way of knowing each trainee's weakness. I was singled out one night during a cold miserable night watching dozens of people including my entire barracks room, most of my boat crew and many within the class I felt confident would make it all the way, quit one after another and sometimes in droves. My thoughts had always been that I would rather die than quit. When told to go back and sink neck deep into the same water that the rest of my class had just vacated by myself,

I knew then and there that my do or die mantra was going to be tested to its nucleus core.

As the single instructor watched nonchalantly as I shivered in a futile attempt to stay warm in the Pacific Ocean South of Imperial Beach near the Mexican border, I had my moment of clarity. I just let go of all thoughts of failing in overcoming the cold and just like that I felt peace and the shivering stopped. I felt like I was in a nirvana moment. Hell could freeze over if needed to convince the instructor I had what it took to achieve against impossible odds or figments of our creative minds.

My mind from that moment forward has always overcome impossible odds. With the Arch Angel Michael moment, it went to another level of achieving the impossible again. You that are reading this work also have that same potential within you.

By reading this book and believing in the unique and amazing miracle of life that you are, awakening and unleashing your own intuitive power is within reach. Will you grasp it now and make it yours?

Michael Jaco
June, 2022

GLOSSARY

Awakening: a sudden recognition or realization of something.

Discipline: the ability to behave in a controlled and calm way even in a difficult or stressful situation; mental self-control used in directing or changing behavior.

Entrainment: the process of synchronization, where vibrations of one object will cause the vibrations of another object to oscillate at the same rate.

Fear: an unpleasant feeling of apprehension or distress caused by the presence or anticipation of danger.

Galactic core: the rotational center of the Milky Way galaxy. It is located about twenty five thousand light years away from the Earth in the direction of the constellations Sagittarius and Scorpius where the Milky Way appears brightest. There is a supermassive black hole at the Galactic Center of the Milky Way.

Intellect: ability to think, reason, and understand.

Intuit: to be aware of or know something without having to think about it or learn it.

Intuition: the state of being aware of or knowing something without having to discover or perceive it, or the ability to do this.

Intuitive: known directly, without being discovered or consciously perceived.

Love: an intense feeling of tender affection and compassion;– everything is encompassed by love and all is for love, starting from loving friends and family, husbands and wives, and eventually reaching the divine love that is the ultimate goal in life.

Pineal gland: a small, cone-shaped organ of the brain that secretes the hormone melatonin into the bloodstream.

Precognitive: denotes a form of extrasensory perception wherein a person is said to perceive information about places or events through paranormal means before they happen.

Prescient: having or showing knowledge of actions or events before they take place.

Quantum physics: a branch of science that deals with discrete, indivisible units of energy called quanta as described by the Quantum Theory. There are five main ideas represented in Quantum Theory: Energy is not continuous, but comes in small, discrete units. The elementary particles behave both like particles *and* like waves. The movement of these particles is inherently random. It is *physically impossible* to know both the position and the momentum of a particle at the same time. The more precisely one is known, the less precise the measurement of the other is. The atomic world is *nothing* like the world we live in.

Reincarnation: in some systems of belief, the cyclical return of a soul to live another life in a new body.

Soul: the complex of human attributes that manifests as consciousness, thought, feeling, and will, regarded as distinct from the physical body.

Spirit: somebody or something that is a divine, inspiring, or animating influence *Spiritual*: relating to the soul or spirit, usually in contrast to material things.

Vortex: a whirling mass of something, especially water or air, that draws everything near it toward its center.

Warrior: somebody who fights or is experienced in warfare; a person who shows or has shown great vigor, courage, or aggressiveness, as in politics or athletics.

WORKS CONSULTED

Ansary, Alex. "The Emerging Sunspot Cycle 24 and a Weakening Magnetic Field." http://www.alexansary.com/Editorial/Sun%20spots%20and%20a%20weakened%20 magnetic%20field.html. February 25, 2009.

Bailey, Alice. *From Intellect to Intuition*. New York: Lucis Publishing Company, 1988.

Bates, Harry and Edmund H. North. *The Day the Earth Stood Still*, DVD, directed by Scott Derrickson. 20th Century Fox, 2008.

Bauval, Robert and Adrian Gilbert. *The Orion Mystery: Unlocking the Secrets of the Pyramids*. New York: Crown Publishers, 1994.

"Climate change hits Mars". The Sunday Times. http://www.timesonline.co.uk/tol/ news/uk/ article1720024.ece. April 29, 2007.

Clow, Barbara Hand. *The Mayan Code: Time Acceleration and Awakening the World Mind*. Rochester, VT: Bear and Company, 2007.

Coppola, Francis Ford and Edmund H. North. *Patton,* DVD, directed by Franklin J. Schaffner (1970; 20th Century Fox, 2001).

Demitriev, Dr. Alexey N. "Planetophysical State of The Earth And Life." Published in Russian, IICA Transactions, Volume 4, 1997. http://www.tmgnow.com/ repository/global/ planetophysical.html.

Eisenhower, Dwight D. *Public Papers of the Presidents of the United States: Dwight D. Eisenhower*. Washington, D C.: National Archives of the US, 1957. pp. 1035-1040.

Emoto, Masaru. *The Hidden Messages in Water,* DVD, I.H.M. General Institute, 2004. "Fire Destroys Johnny Cash's Nashville Home." CBS News. http://www. cbsnews.com/ stories/2007/04/10/entertainment/main2668658.shtml. April 10, 2007.

Hapgood, Charles. *Maps of the Ancient Sea Kings*. London: Turnstone Books, 1979.

Hancock, Graham and Robert Bauval. *The Message of the Sphinx: A Quest for the Hidden Legacy of Mankind*. New York: Crown Publishers, 1996.

Hawkins, David. *Power vs. Force: The Hidden Determinants of Human Behavior*. Carlsbad, CA: Hay House, 2002.

Hicks, Esther and Jerry Hicks. *The Law of Attraction: The Basic of the Teachings of Abraham*. Carlsbad, CA: Hay House. 2006.

Hoagland, Richard and David Wilcock. "Interplanetary 'Day After Tomorrow'? Parts 1,2 & 3." 2004, http://www.enterprisemission.com/_articles/05-14-2004_ Interplanetary_Part_1/ Interplanetary_1.html.

Jenkins, John Major. *Galactic Alignment: The Transformation of Consciousness According to Mayan, Egyptian, and Vedic Traditions.* Rochester, VT: Bear & Company, 2002.

Lombardi, Candace. "NASA images show thinning Arctic sea ice." *CNET.* http:// news.cnet.com/ 8301-11128_3-10213891-54.html. April 7, 2009.

Marshall, Edison. *The Vikings,* DVD, directed by Richard Fleisher. MGM, 2002.

Martinez, Carolina and Gary Galluzzo. "Scientists Find That Saturn's Rotation Period is a Puzzle". Nasa.gov. http://www.nasa.gov/mission_pages/cassini/media/ cassini-062804.html. June 28, 2004.

McTaggart, Lynne. *The Field Updated Ed: The Quest for the Secret Force of the Universe.* New York: HarperCollins, 2008.

The Intention Experiment: Using Your Thoughts to Change Your Life and the World. New York: Free Press, 2008.

Pool, Robert Roy and Jonathan Hensleigh. *Armageddon,* DVD, directed by Michael Bay. Buena Vista Home Entertainment/Touchstone, 1999.

Ravilious Kate. "Mars Melt Hints at Solar, Not Human, Cause for Warming, Scientist Says." *National Geographic.* http://news.nationalgeographic.com/ news/2007/02/070228-mars- warming.html. February 28, 2007.

Schumann Resonance. *http://www.schumanwaves.com.*

"Vatican gives blessing to belief in aliens". CTV.ca. http://www.ctv.ca/servlet/ ArticleNews/ story/CTVNews/20080514/ aliens_vatican_080514/20080514?h ub=SciTech. May14, 2008. Velikovsky, Immanuel. *Worlds in Collision.* New York: The Macmillan Company, 1950.

Waller, Douglas C. *The Commandos: The Inside Story of America's Secret Soldiers.* New York: Bantam Dell Publishing Group, 1995.

Walsch, Neale Donald. *Home with God: In a Life That Never Ends.* Memphis, TN: Atria, 2007. Weiss, Brian L. *Same Soul, Many Bodies: Discovering the Healing Power of Future Lives Through Progression Therapy.* New York: Free Press, 2004.

White, John. *Pole Shift: Predictions and Prophecies of the Ultimate Disaster.* Virginia Beach, VA: A.R.E. Press, 1985.

RECOMMENDED RESOURCES

Bird, Christopher and Peter Tompkins. *The Secret Life of Plants*. New York: HarperCollins Publishers, 1989.

Braden, Gregg. *Fractal Time: The secret of 2012 and a New World Age*. Carlsbad, CA: Hay House, 2009.

Chasse, Betsy et al. *What the Bleep Do We Know?*, DVD, directed by Betsy Chasse and Mark Vicente (2004; 20th Century Fox, 2005.

Chopra, Deepak and Wayne Dyer. *Creating your world the way you really want it to be*: Audiobook. Carlsbad, CA: Hay House Audio Books, 1998.

Hess, Hermann. *Siddhartha*. Winnetka, CA: Norilana Books, 2007.

"Jill Bolte Taylor's stroke of insight." Filmed Feb 2008; Posted Mar 2008,TED.com, http://www.ted.com/index.php/talks/jill_bolte_taylor_s_powerful_stroke_of_insight.html. June 27, 2009.

Keene, Jeffrey J., *Someone Else's Yesterday: The Confederate General and Connecticut Yankee: A Past Life Revealed*. Nevada City, CA: Blue Dolphin Publishing, 2003.

Lipton, Bruce. *The Biology of Belief: Unleashing the Power of Consciousness, Matter, & Miracles*. Carlsbad, CA: Hay House, 2008.

Marcinko, Richard. *Rogue Warrior*. New York: Simon & Schuster, 1993.

Pressfield, Steven. *Gates Of Fire: An Epic Novel of the Battle of Thermopylae*. New York: Bantam Dell Publishing Group, 2005.

Ruiz, Don Miguel. *The Four Agreements: A Practical Guide to Personal Freedom, A Toltec Wisdom Book*. San Rafael, CA: Amber-Allen Publishing, 2001.

Stearn, Jess. Edgar Cayce: *The Sleeping Prophet*. New York: Bantam Dell Publishing Group, 1989.

The Secret, DVD, directed by Drew Heriot. Prime Time Productions, 2006.

Tolle, Eckhart. *A New Earth: Awakening to Your Life's Purpose*. New York: Penguin Group, 2008; *The Power of Now: A Guide to Spiritual Enlightenment*. Novato, CA: New World Library, 2004.

Trevinian. *Shibumi: A Novel*. New York: Crown Publishing Group, 2005.

Walsch, Neale Donald. *Conversations with God: An Uncommon Dialogue: Book 1*. Kirkwood, NY: Putnam Publishing Group, 1996; *Conversations with God: An Uncommon Dialogue: Book 2*. Charlottesville, VA: Hampton Roads Publishing Company, 1997; *Conversations with God: An Uncommon Dialogue: Book 3*. Charlottesville, VA: Hampton Roads Publishing Company, 1998.

Williamson, Marianne. *A Return to Love: Reflections on the Principles of "A Course in Miracles."* New York: HarperCollins Publishers, 1996.

ABOUT THE AUTHOR

Michael Jaco was born and raised in Columbia, South Carolina. He enlisted in the United States Navy in November 1978 and started his career as a Navy Hard Hat Diver. He volunteered for Basic Underwater Demolition/Sea Air and Land (BUD/S) training in August 1981. He completed BUD/S training 6 months later with class 116 in February 1982. He served with distinction as a Navy SEAL with the following commands:

UDT-12, SEAL TEAMS – 3, 4, 5, & 6 Naval Special Warfare Development Group Naval Special Warfare Training Center (BUD/S/1st Phase); Naval Special Warfare Training Center (Advanced Training); Naval Special Warfare Unit - 1 (Guam); United States Naval Academy. Upon leaving the US Navy in December 2002 he has served as a High Risk Security Contractor for over 8 years. Providing security leadership for 40 different contracts in the most violent war torn areas of the world.

❖

Navy Seal Team Six operator and CIA security operative with expert intuitive abilities developed over 35 years of extensive combat experience.

With over 20 years of experience as an Intuitive, Remote Viewer and Remote Influencer in diverse environments including combat Michael has expertly honed his skills in the higher consciousness realms.

As a master training specialist Michael has trained thousands of people in extremely high levels of personal development.

Michael's mission and life focus is to help anyone quickly and easily develop the skills for success in all aspects of human achievement.

Connect with Michael online at:
http://www.michaeljaco.com

Cover and book design by Mark J. Maxam, designer

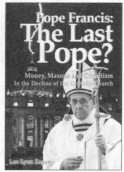

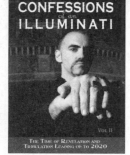
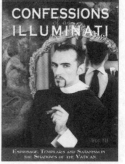
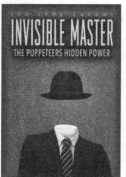

SACRED PLACES SERIES / WORLD STOMPERS

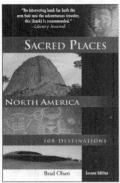

Sacred Places North America: 108 Destinations

– 2nd EDITION; by Brad Olsen

This comprehensive travel guide examines North America's most sacred sites for spiritually attuned explorers. Spirituality & Health reviewed: "The book is filled with fascinating archeological, geological, and historical material. These 108 sacred places in the United States, Canada, and Hawaii offer ample opportunity for questing by spiritual seekers."

$19.95 :: 408 pages   **paperback: 978-1888729139**

... all Ebooks priced at $9.99

Kindle: 978-1888729252; PDF: 973-1888729191
ePub: 978-1888729337

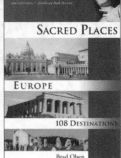

Sacred Places Europe:
108 Destinations – by Brad Olsen

This guide to European holy sites examines the most significant locations that shaped the religious consciousness of Western civilization. Travel to Europe for 108 uplifting destinations that helped define religion and spirituality in the Western Hemisphere. From Paleolithic cave art and Neolithic megaliths, to New Age temples, this is an impartial guide book many millennium in the making.

$19.95 :: 344 pages   paperback: 978-1888729122

... all Ebooks priced at $9.99

Kindle: 978-1888729245; PDF: 978-1888729184
ePub: 978-1888729320

Sacred Places of Goddess: 108 Destinations – by Karen Tate

Readers will be escorted on a pilgrimage that reawakens, rethinks, and reveals the Divine Feminine in a multitude of sacred locations on every continent. Meticulously researched, clearly written and comprehensively documented, this book explores the rich tapestry of Goddess worship from prehistoric cultures to modern academic theories.

$19.95 :: 424 pages   **paperback: 978-1888729115**

... all Ebooks priced at $9.99

Kindle: 978-1888729269; PDF: 973-1888729177
ePub: 978-1888729344

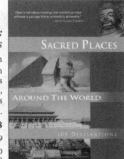

Sacred Places Around the World:
108 Destinations

– 2nd EDITION; by Brad Olsen

The mystical comes alive in this exciting compilation of 108 beloved holy destinations. World travelers and armchair tourists who want to explore the mythology and archaeology of the ruins, sanctuaries, mountains, lost cities, and temples of ancient civilizations will find this guide ideal.

$17.95 :: 288 pages   paperback: 978-1888729108

... all Ebooks priced at $8.99

Kindle: 978-1888729238; PDF: 978-1888729160
ePub: 978-1888729313

World Stompers:
A Global Travel Manifesto

– 5th EDITION; by Brad Olsen

Here is a travel guide written specifically to assist and motivate young readers to travel the world. When you are ready to leave your day job, load up your backpack and head out to distant lands for extended periods of time, Brad Olsen's "Travel Classic" will lend a helping hand.

$17.95 :: 288 pages   **paperback: 978-1888729054**

... all Ebooks priced at $8.99

Kindle: 978-1888729276; PDF: 978-1888729061
ePub: 978-1888729351

THE ESOTERIC SERIES FROM CCC PUBLISHING

Beyond Esoteric:
Escaping Prison Planet
– by Brad Olsen

Nothing in this world works the way we are led to believe it does; there is always more to the story. Be aware that there is a war being waged for your body, mind and soul. Owners of corporations have taken over governments in a new form of Fascism that now incorporates high technology and artificial intelligence. The survival of the human race may depend on breaking the Truth Embargo, that is, exposing the Big Lie.

$19.95 :: 480 pages; paperback: 978-1888729740

... all eBooks priced $9.99

All ebook ISBN versions: 978-1888729757

Modern Esoteric:
Beyond our Senses
– 2nd EDITION; by Brad Olsen

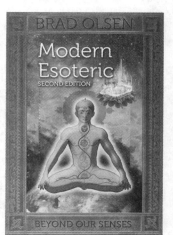

Organized into three sections (Lifeology, Control and Thrive), Modern Esoteric: Beyond Our Senses by World Explorer magazine editor Brad Olsen examines the flaws in ancient and modern history, plus explains how esoteric knowledge, conspiracy theories, and fringe subjects can be used to help change the dead-end course we humans seem to be blindly running ourselves into.

$17.95 :: 480 pages; paperback: 978-1888729504

... all eBooks priced $9.99

Kindle: 978-1888729856 • PDF: 978-1888729832 • ePub: 978-1888729849

Future Esoteric:
The Unseen Realms
– 2nd EDITION; by Brad Olsen

Things are not always as they appear. For the past century forbidden subjects such as UFOs, human abductions, secret space programs, suppressed free energy devices and other fantastic notions have tested the human mind, forcing it to decipher fact from fiction. But is there a common thread? As sites like WikiLeaks and their founders try to unveil war secrets and covert black operations, international governments have little-by-little begun exposing what they've tried for years to keep hidden. Chronicling what he calls the "alternative narrative," Brad Olsen gets down to the middle of it all.

$17.95 :: 416 pages; paperback: 978-1888729788

... all eBooks priced $9.99

Kindle: 978-1888729801 • PDF: 978-1888729795 • ePub: 978-1888729818

CCC Publishing is distributed by Independent Publishers Group (800) 888-4741, www.IPGBook.com
Follow us on: www.EsotericSeries.com & www.Facebook.com/ccc.publishing • www.CCCPublishing.com
features the content of all of our books online, plus blogs, ebooks & discounts